taste of Greece

taste of Greece

irresistible dishes of the sun-soaked Eastern Mediterranean

joanna farrow and jacqueline clarke

This edition published by Hermes House in 2002

Hermes House is an imprint of
Anness Publishing Limited
Hermes House
88–89 Blackfriars Road
London SE1 8HA

A CIP catalogue record for this book is available from the British Library.

Publisher: Joanna Lorenz
Senior Cookery Editor: Linda Fraser
Designers: Nigel Partridge and Ian Sandom
Photography and styling: Michelle Garrett, assisted by Dulce Riberio
Food for photography: Jacqueline Clark and Joanna Farrow
Illustrator: Anna Koska
Production Controller: Joanna King

Front cover shows a variation on Stuffed Squid, for recipe see page 48

Previously published as *Recipes from a Greek Kitchen*

1 3 5 7 9 10 8 6 4 2

NOTES

For all recipes, quantities are given in both metric and imperial measures and, where appropriate, measures are also given in standard cups and spoons. Follow one set, but not a mixture because they are not interchangeable.

Standard spoon and cup measurements are level.
1 tsp = 5ml, 1 tbsp = 15ml, 1 cup = 250ml/8fl oz

Medium eggs should be used unless otherwise stated.

Australian standard tablespoons are 20ml. Australian readers should use 3 tsp in place of 1 tbsp for measuring small quantities of gelatine, cornflour, salt etc.

Contents

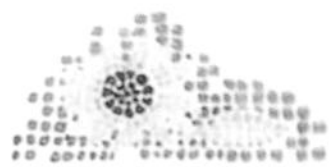

INTRODUCTION

The countries of the eastern Mediterranean - Greece, Turkey, Cyprus, Egypt - and the Middle East share a cuisine based on the influence of the sea, the climate and the history of the area. It is a fascinating mix of simply cooked foods based on wonderful fresh ingredients whose flavours are drawn out by the hot sun, rice and minced meat dishes designed to make a substantial meal out of inexpensive or scarce ingredients, and recipes incorporating exotic spices and flavourings.

In ancient times the area surrounding the Mediterranean Sea was colonized by the Phoenicians, Greeks and Romans, who cultivated wheat, olives and grapes. These, in turn, became bread, oil and wine, three components that are still very important in today's Mediterranean diet. With the building of ships came import and export, with the result that spices and flavourings were introduced through North Africa and Arabia. Saffron, cloves, chillies, ginger and allspice are still popular all over the Mediterranean, appearing in both sweet and savoury dishes.

A market stall in southern Turkey with an abundance of tomatoes, onions, potatoes and grapes.

This exotic influence, together with the fact that our impressions of the Eastern Mediterranean are largely formed by visits there during the summer, make it difficult to imagine that the agriculture of the region does suffer from bad weather. However, drought on the land and storms at sea do ruin crops and the fisherman's catch. Because of this, the most basic foods are, even today, a celebration of life to the Greek people. Bread is an important staple and always accompanies a meal, be it a bowl of soup or a platter of grilled fish.

A Greek street market is a fascinating scene, full of colour and bustle. Greek vegetables have an inviting irregularity about them: uneven colourings, knobbly skins and unsymmetrical shapes are a sure indication that the flesh inside will be full of flavour, far superior to the mass-produced, artificially grown produce of colder climates. The dishes cooked using them are a joy to eat, and even the simplest tossed salad of tomatoes and leaves, sprinkled with olive oil and seasoning, is worthy of serving solo.

In the Eastern Mediterranean, local and specialized variations of a mezze (a spread of appetizers) are popular with both locals and visitors, and, in Greece, can be accompanied by either ouzo or wine. Sheep's and goat's

yogurt are hung to produce thickened cheeses that are bottled in spiced olive oil; these are delicious spread on warm toast. Dressed tomatoes, fried halloumi or kefalotyri cheese drizzled with lemon juice and pepper, and a bowl of garlic-flavoured Greek yogurt are often served as a lavish first course.

The Mediterranean Sea is tiny in relation to the world's larger seas and oceans. It is also relatively shallow, warm, low in natural food supplies and more polluted. Despite all these factors, the Mediterranean has hundreds of different species of fish and crustacea. A visit to a Greek taverna illustrates how this freshly caught fish, cooked simply, can be quite unbeatable. Perfectly fresh fish, grilled with a basting of olive oil, garlic and herbs, needs little more embellishment, except perhaps a crisp salad and light wine. On a more elaborate scale, fish stews and soups are typical all around the Mediterranean.

Unlike the vegetable and fish dishes, however, meat recipes are less abundant. The countryside around the Mediterranean can be quite harsh, with no lush, green fields for animals to graze. Lamb and goat are favourite meats. The meat of the young kid is particularly popular in parts of Greece, in Corsica and the Middle East. The Greek Orthodox Church formerly had strict rules concerning "lean" days, when meat was forbidden, so many special feast dishes using meat were created to celebrate the end of these regular fasts.

The day's catch is brought home to Crete packed in salt.

The countries surrounding the Mediterranean produce a seemingly inexhaustible quantity and variety of grains and pulses. Wheat, the most ancient cereal grown in the region, predominates. Wheat flour is also used to make the highly popular filo pastries of Greece, Turkey, Lebanon and North Africa. It is skillfully shaped and stretched to form a transparent sheet that is then brushed with olive oil or melted butter and folded into layers. When cooked, it resembles a very light and crisp puff pastry. Filo is used in many sweet or savoury classics such as the Middle Eastern chicken and apricot pie.

Shopping for vegetables and local news in a Turkish market.

Desserts produced in Greece and elsewhere in the Mediterranean take full advantage of the glorious abundance of fresh fruits. For a special occasion, a colourful selection of seasonal fruits such as figs, plums, apricots, peaches, melons and cherries makes a stunning finale. These can be arranged on a platter lined with vine or fig leaves, some fruits cut open decoratively, and the whole platter scattered with crushed ice. Honey is plentiful and therefore much favoured as a sweetener, often teamed with nuts and dates. The most popular nuts are almonds, pistachios and pine nuts, as they are native to the region.

Fresh salads, simply prepared main courses, spiced grains, delicious breads and fruit flavoured with nuts and honey – these are the tastes of Greece and the Eastern Mediterranean to be enjoyed to their full through the recipes in this delicious collection.

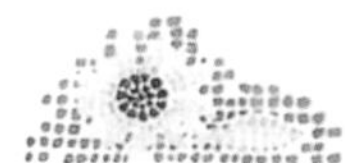

Ingredients

Aubergines
Although aubergines originated from Asia, they feature in dishes from Greece and every Mediterranean country. There are many different varieties, including green, white and yellow, but the plump purple variety is the most common. Look for firm, taut, shiny-skinned specimens with green stalks. Aubergines are sometimes salted and drained before cooking, which helps to extract bitter juices and makes them absorb less oil during cooking.

Cheese
The Greek cheeses most widely available outside Greece are feta and halloumi. Feta is made from goat's milk and is a popular ingredient in salads. Halloumi is generally made from ewe's milk and is often fried, then served with lemon juice and pepper.

Chick-peas
This pulse looks like a pale golden hazelnut and is sold either dried or ready cooked. Chick-peas have a nutty flavour and are widely used in stews from North Africa to Spain. In Greece and Turkey they are puréed with olive oil to produce hummus, a delicious dip. Soak them for up to 4 hours, depending on how old they are, in order to tenderize them.

Cumin Seeds
These dark, spindly-shaped seeds are often married with coriander when making the spicy dishes that are typical of the Eastern Mediterranean and North Africa. They are also ground to make tahini.

Dates
Although fresh dates are quite widely available, imported from Egypt, Israel and California, the dried variety remains invaluable. Fresh dates should be plump and slightly wrinkled. They have a rich, honey-like flavour and dense texture.

Fennel
This white bulb of overlapping leaves and green, feathery fronds has a fresh aniseed flavour and can be eaten cooked or raw. Its flavour complements fish and chicken very well. Choose firm, rounded bulbs, and use the fronds for garnishing.

Figs
This fruit is associated with Greece and all the Mediterranean countries. Different varieties vary in colour, from dark purple to green to a golden yellow, but all are made up of hundreds of tiny seeds, surrounded by soft pink flesh that is perfectly edible. Choose firm unblemished figs, which just yield to the touch.

Fresh herbs
Huge bundles of fresh coriander are a familiar sight in Eastern Mediterranean markets, their warm, pungent aroma rising at the merest touch. The leaves impart a distinctive flavour to soups, stews, sauces and spicy dishes when added towards the end of cooking. They are also used sparingly in salads and yogurt dishes. Mint also features in many recipes as an integral part and as a garnish, its fresh taste adding zest to creamy dishes and pulses. Parsley, dill, oregano, basil and many other fresh herbs all play an important part.

Garlic
Sold in "strings" or as separate bulbs, the main consideration when buying garlic is that the cloves are plump and firm. Used crushed, sliced or even whole, garlic develops a smooth, gentle flavour with long, slow cooking. Used raw in salads, mayonnaise and sauce, garlic has a hot, fierce impact.

Harissa
A fiery hot paste made from a blend of chillies, garlic, cumin, coriander and cayenne. It can be bought in small jars.

Mussels
Mussels usually need to be scrubbed and have the beard – the hairy tuft attached to the shell – removed. Any open mussels should be discarded before cooking if they do not close after a sharp tap. Mussels vary in size, and the shell can be blue-black to dappled brown. They are easy to cook – just steam for a few minutes in a covered pan.

Olive Oil
Together with its healthy qualities, olive oil is indispensable to Greek

cooking for its fine, nutty flavour. The richest oil comes from the first cold pressing of the olives, producing a golden green "virgin" oil.

OLIVES
The fruit of one of the earliest known trees native to the Mediterranean. There are hundreds of varieties, differing widely in size, quality and taste. Colour depends purely on ripeness – the fruit changes from yellow to green, violet, purple, brown and finally black when fully ripened. Fresh olives are picked at the desired stage of ripeness, then soaked in water, bruised and immersed in brine to produce the familiar-tasting result. They can be bought whole or pitted, sometimes stuffed with peppers, anchovies or nuts, or bottled with flavourings such as garlic, coriander, chilli and herbs.

PEPPERS
In Greece, Turkey and the Middle East sweet peppers are served stuffed, filled with couscous, rice, herbs, spices, dried fruits, nuts, cheese and sometimes meat. Another way of making the most of the flavour of sweet peppers is to grill them until the skins are charred, rub off and discard the skins, then marinate the peppers in olive oil.

PINE NUTS
These little nuts are used in both sweet and savoury dishes. They are often served with marinated vegetables, and are an important ingredient in sweet pastries.

PRAWNS
These vary enormously in size: the classic Mediterranean prawn is large, about 20cm/8in. When prawns are cooked over a fierce heat, such as a barbecue, the shell is often left on to protect the flesh from charring.

SEA BASS
This is quite an expensive fish and is usually sold and cooked whole. The flesh is soft and delicate and needs careful attention when cooking. Methods include poaching, steaming, grilling and baking.

SQUID
Squid vary in size, from the tiny specimens that can be eaten whole, to the larger varieties, which are good for stuffing, grilling or stewing. The flesh is sweet and tender when either cooked briefly over a fierce heat or given a long cooking over a low heat.

TAHINI
A smooth oily paste ground from sesame seeds and used to give a nutty flavour to Middle Eastern dishes.

TUNA
A large oily fish belonging to the same family as mackerel. The flesh, which is sold in steaks or large pieces, is dark red and very dense, and has a tendency to dry out when cooked. Marinating before cooking helps to keep the flesh moist, as does basting frequently while cooking. Tuna can be baked, fried, grilled or stewed.

YOGURT
This live dairy product (pasteurized milk combined with two beneficial bacteria) is a typical ingredient in the cuisines of the Eastern Mediterranean and is used to make soft cheese. Greek yogurt, made from either sheep or cow's milk, is thick and creamy.

SOUPS AND STARTERS

Soups can be light and refreshing like Avgolemono or substantial enough, when eaten with bread, to make a nourishing meal, such as Green Lentil Soup. Cold soups are a feature of the cuisine of the Eastern Mediterranean – they are yogurt-based, usually mixed with cucumber and garlic, and spiked with mint. Starters are also a speciality of this area and are made from all types of food, both cooked and uncooked. Called "mezze" or "mezedes", they form an important part of the meal. The selection in this chapter presents recipes for cheese, seafood and vegetables as a taster in itself.

SPICED MUSSEL SOUP

Chunky and colourful, this Turkish fish soup is like a chowder in its consistency. It's flavoured with harissa sauce, more familiar in North African cookery.

1.5kg/3–3½lb fresh mussels
150ml/¼ pint/⅔ cup white wine
3 tomatoes
30ml/2 tbsp olive oil
1 onion, finely chopped
2 garlic cloves, crushed
2 celery sticks, thinly sliced
bunch of spring onions, thinly sliced
1 potato, diced
7.5ml/1½ tsp harissa sauce
45ml/3 tbsp chopped fresh parsley
ground black pepper
thick yogurt, to serve (optional)

SERVES 6

1 Scrub the mussels, discarding any damaged ones or any open ones that do not close when tapped with a knife.

2 Bring the wine to the boil in a large saucepan. Add the mussels and cover with a lid. Cook for 4–5 minutes until the mussels have opened wide. Discard any mussels that remain closed. Drain the mussels, reserving the cooking liquid. Reserve a few mussels in their shells for garnish and shell the rest.

3 Peel the tomatoes and dice them. Heat the oil in a pan and fry the onion, garlic, celery and spring onions for 5 minutes.

4 Add the shelled mussels, reserved liquid, potato, harissa sauce and tomatoes. Bring just to the boil, reduce the heat and cover. Simmer gently for 25 minutes, or until the potatoes are breaking up.

5 Stir in the parsley and pepper and add the reserved mussels. Heat through for 1 minute. Serve hot with a spoonful of yogurt, if you like.

GREEN LENTIL SOUP

Lentil soup is an Eastern Mediterranean classic, varying in its spiciness according to region. Red or puy lentils make an equally good substitute for the green lentils used here.

225g/8oz/1 cup green lentils
75ml/5 tbsp olive oil
3 onions, finely chopped
2 garlic cloves, thinly sliced
10ml/2 tsp cumin seeds, crushed
1.5ml/¼ tsp ground turmeric
600ml/1 pint/2½ cups chicken or vegetable stock
salt and ground black pepper
30ml/2 tbsp roughly chopped fresh coriander, to finish

SERVES 4–6

1 Put the lentils in a saucepan and cover with cold water. Bring to the boil and boil rapidly for 10 minutes. Drain.

2 Heat 30ml/2 tbsp of the oil in a pan and fry two of the onions with the garlic, cumin and turmeric for 3 minutes, stirring. Add the lentils, stock and 600ml/1 pint/2½ cups water. Bring to the boil, reduce the heat, cover and simmer gently for 30 minutes, until the lentils are soft.

3 Fry the third onion in the remaining oil until golden.

4 Use a potato masher to lightly mash the lentils and make the soup pulpy. Reheat gently and season with salt and pepper to taste. Pour the soup into bowls. Stir the fresh coriander into the fried onion and scatter over the soup. Serve with warm bread.

SPICY PUMPKIN SOUP

Pumpkin is popular all over the Mediterranean and it's an important ingredient in Middle Eastern cookery, from which this soup is inspired. Ginger and cumin give the soup its spicy flavour.

900g/2lb pumpkin, peeled and seeds removed
30ml/2 tbsp olive oil
2 leeks, trimmed and sliced
1 garlic clove, crushed
5ml/1 tsp ground ginger
5ml/1 tsp ground cumin
900ml/1½ pints/3¾ cups chicken stock
salt and ground black pepper
coriander leaves, to garnish
60ml/4 tbsp natural yogurt, to serve

SERVES 4

1 Cut the pumpkin into chunks. Heat the oil in a large pan and add the leeks and garlic. Cook gently until softened.

2 Add the ginger and cumin and cook, stirring, for a further minute. Add the pumpkin and the chicken stock and season with salt and pepper. Bring to the boil and simmer for 30 minutes, until the pumpkin is tender. Process the soup, in batches if necessary, in a blender or food processor.

3 Reheat the soup and serve in warmed individual bowls, with a swirl of yogurt and a garnish of coriander leaves.

MIDDLE EASTERN YOGURT AND CUCUMBER SOUP

Yogurt is used extensively in Middle Eastern cookery, and it is usually made at home. Sometimes it is added at the end of cooking a dish, to prevent it from curdling, but in this cold soup the yogurt is one of the basic ingredients.

1 large cucumber, peeled
300ml/½ pint/1¼ cups single cream
150ml/¼ pint/⅔ cup natural yogurt
2 garlic cloves, crushed
30ml/2 tbsp white wine vinegar
15ml/1 tbsp chopped fresh mint
salt and ground black pepper
sprigs of mint, to garnish

SERVES 4

1 Grate the cucumber coarsely. Place in a bowl with the cream, yogurt, garlic, vinegar and mint. Stir well and season to taste.

2 Chill for at least 2 hours before serving. Just before serving, stir the soup again. Pour into individual bowls and garnish with mint sprigs.

AVGOLEMONO

This is the most popular of Greek soups. The name means egg and lemon, the two important ingredients, which produce a light, nourishing soup. Orzo is Greek, rice-shaped pasta, but you can use any small shape.

1.75 litres/3 pints/7½ cups chicken stock
115g/4oz/½ cup orzo pasta
3 eggs
juice of 1 large lemon
salt and ground black pepper
lemon slices, to garnish

SERVES 4–6

1 Pour the stock into a large pan, and bring to the boil. Add the pasta and cook for 5 minutes.

2 Beat the eggs until frothy, then add the lemon juice and a tablespoon of cold water. Slowly stir in a ladleful of the hot chicken stock, then add one or two more. Return this mixture to the pan, off the heat and stir well. Season with salt and pepper and serve at once, garnished with lemon slices. (Do not let the soup boil once the eggs have been added or it will curdle.)

FRESH TOMATO SOUP

Intensely flavoured sun-ripened tomatoes need little embellishment in this fresh-tasting soup. If you buy from the supermarket, choose the ripest looking ones and add the amount of sugar and vinegar necessary, depending on their natural sweetness. On a hot day this soup is also delicious chilled.

1.5kg/3–3½lb ripe tomatoes
400ml/14fl oz/1⅔ cups chicken or vegetable stock
45ml/3 tbsp sun-dried tomato paste
0–45ml/2–3 tbsp balsamic vinegar
10–15ml/2–3 tsp caster sugar
small handful basil leaves
salt and ground black pepper
basil leaves, to garnish
toasted cheese croûtes and crème fraîche, to serve

SERVES 6

1 Plunge the tomatoes into boiling water for 30 seconds, then refresh in cold water. Peel away the skins and quarter the tomatoes. Put them in a large saucepan and pour over the chicken or vegetable stock. Bring just to the boil, reduce the heat, cover and simmer gently for 10 minutes until the tomatoes are pulpy.

2 Stir in the tomato paste, vinegar, sugar and basil. Season with salt and pepper, then cook gently, stirring, for 2 minutes. Process the soup in a blender or food processor, then return to the pan and reheat gently. Serve in bowls topped with one or two toasted cheese croûtes and a spoonful of crème fraîche, garnished with basil leaves.

YOGURT CHEESE IN OLIVE OIL

Sheep's milk is widely used in cheese making in the Eastern Mediterranean, particularly in Greece where sheep's yogurt is hung in muslin to drain off the whey before patting into balls of soft cheese. Here it's bottled in olive oil with chilli and herbs – an appropriate gift for a "foodie" friend.

750g/1¾lb Greek sheep's yogurt
2.5ml/½ tsp salt
10ml/2 tsp crushed dried chillies or chilli powder
15ml/1 tbsp chopped fresh rosemary
15ml/1 tbsp chopped fresh thyme or oregano
about 300ml/½ pint/1¼ cups olive oil, preferably garlic-flavoured

FILLS TWO 450G/1LB JARS

1 Sterilize a 30cm/12in square of muslin by steeping it in boiling water. Drain and lay over a large plate. Mix the yogurt with the salt and tip on to the centre of the muslin. Bring up the sides of the muslin and tie firmly with string.

2 Hang the bag on a kitchen cupboard handle or suitable position where the bag can be suspended with a bowl underneath to catch the whey. Leave for 2–3 days until the yogurt stops dripping.

3 Sterilize two 450g/1lb glass preserving or jam jars by heating them in the oven at 150°C/300°F/Gas 2 for 15 minutes.

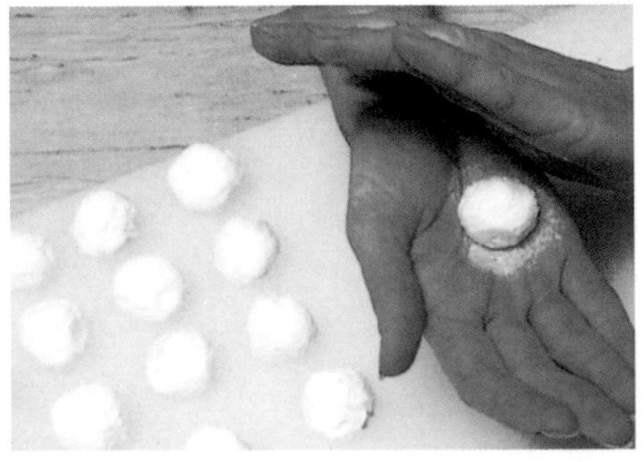

4 Mix together the chilli and herbs. Take teaspoonfuls of the cheese and roll into balls with your hands. Lower into the jars, sprinkling each layer with the herb mixture.

5 Pour the oil over the cheese until completely covered. Store in the fridge for up to 3 weeks.

6 To serve the cheese, spoon out of the jars with a little of the flavoured olive oil and spread on to lightly toasted bread.

Cook's Tip

If your kitchen is particularly warm, find a cooler place to suspend the cheese. Alternatively, drain the cheese in the fridge, suspending the bag from one of the shelves.

SAUTÉED MUSSELS WITH GARLIC AND HERBS

These mussels are served without their shells, in a delicious paprika flavoured sauce. Eat them with cocktail sticks.

900g/2lb fresh mussels
1 lemon slice
90ml/6 tbsp olive oil
2 shallots, finely chopped
1 garlic clove, finely chopped
15ml/1 tbsp chopped fresh parsley
2.5ml/½ tsp sweet paprika
1.5ml/¼ tsp dried chilli flakes

SERVES 4

1 Scrub the mussels, discarding any damaged ones that do not close when tapped with a knife. Put the mussels in a large pan, with 250ml/8fl oz/1 cup water, and the slice of lemon. Bring to the boil for 3–4 minutes and remove the mussels as they open. Discard any that remain closed. Take the mussels out of the shells and drain on kitchen paper.

2 Heat the oil in a sauté pan, add the mussels, and cook, stirring, for a minute. Remove from the pan. Add the shallots and garlic and cook, covered, over a low heat, for about 5 minutes, until soft. Remove from the heat and stir in the parsley, paprika and chilli. Return to the heat and stir in the mussels with any juices. Cook briefly. Remove from the heat and cover for a minute or two, to let the flavours mingle, before serving.

MARINATED BABY AUBERGINES WITH RAISINS AND PINE NUTS

Aubergines are popular in all the Mediterranean countries. Grilled vegetables which are then cooled in an oil and vinegar marinade are a typical starter. Make this recipe a day in advance, to allow the sour and sweet flavours to develop.

12 baby aubergines, halved lengthways
250ml/8fl oz/1 cup extra virgin olive oil
juice of 1 lemon
10ml/2tsp red wine vinegar
3 cloves
25g/1oz/⅓ cup pine nuts
25g/1oz/2 tbsp raisins
15ml/1 tbsp granulated sugar
1 bay leaf
large pinch of dried chilli flakes
salt and ground black pepper

SERVES 4

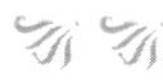

1 Preheat the grill to high. Place the aubergines, cut side up, in the grill pan and brush with a little of the olive oil. Grill for 10 minutes, until slightly blackened, turning them over half way through cooking.

2 To make the marinade, put the remaining olive oil, the lemon juice, vinegar, cloves, pine nuts, raisins, sugar and bay leaf in a jug. Add the chilli flakes and salt and pepper and mix well.

3 Place the hot aubergines in an earthenware or glass bowl, and pour over the marinade. Leave to cool, turning the aubergines once or twice. Serve cold.

GRILLED VEGETABLE TERRINE

A colourful, layered terrine, using all the vegetables associated with the Mediterranean.

2 large red peppers, quartered, cored and seeded
2 large yellow peppers, quartered, cored and seeded
1 large aubergine, sliced lengthways
2 large courgettes, sliced lengthways
90ml/6 tbsp olive oil
1 large red onion, thinly sliced
75g/3oz/½ cup raisins
15ml/1 tbsp tomato purée
15ml/1 tbsp red wine vinegar
400ml/14fl oz/1⅔ cups tomato juice
15g/½oz/2 tbsp powdered gelatine
fresh basil leaves, to garnish

FOR THE DRESSING
90ml/6 tbsp extra virgin olive oil
30ml/2 tbsp red wine vinegar
salt and ground black pepper

SERVES 6

1 Place the prepared red and yellow peppers skin side up under a hot grill and cook until the skins are blackened. Transfer to a bowl and cover with a plate. Leave to cool.

2 Arrange the aubergine and courgette slices on separate baking sheets. Brush them with a little oil and cook under the grill, turning occasionally, until tender and golden.

3 Heat the remaining olive oil in a frying pan, and add the sliced onion, raisins, tomato purée and red wine vinegar. Cook gently until soft and syrupy. Leave to cool in the frying pan.

4 Line a 1.75 litre/3 pint/7½ cup terrine with clear film, (it helps to lightly oil the terrine first) leaving a little hanging over the sides.

5 Pour half the tomato juice into a saucepan, and sprinkle with the gelatine. Dissolve gently over a low heat, stirring.

6 Place a layer of red peppers in the bottom of the terrine, and pour in enough of the tomato juice with gelatine to cover. Continue layering the aubergine, courgettes, yellow peppers and onion mixture, finishing with another layer of red peppers. Pour tomato juice over each layer of vegetables.

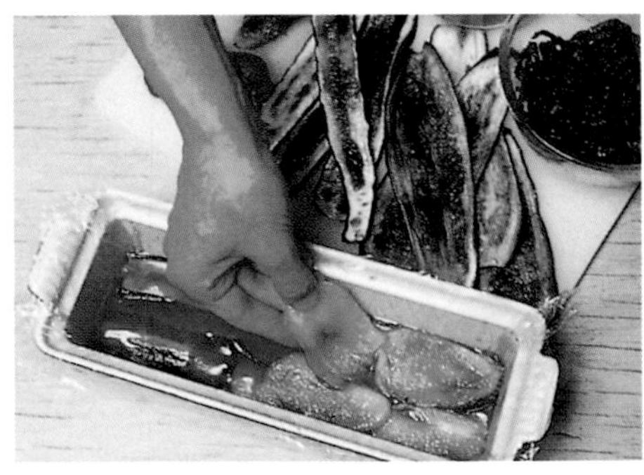

7 Add the remaining tomato juice to any left in the pan, and pour into the terrine. Give it a sharp tap, to disperse the juice. Cover the terrine and chill until set.

8 To make the dressing, whisk together the oil and vinegar, and season. Turn out the terrine and remove the clear film. Serve in thick slices, drizzled with dressing. Garnish with basil leaves.

Salads and Vegetables

The climate of Greece has ensured that salads and cold cooked vegetable dishes have always been popular. Cheese and yogurt are often mixed in with salad vegetables, as in the very popular Greek Salad or in the delicious Halloumi and Grape Salad where the cheese is fried before being added. Stuffed vegetables are greatly loved in Greece, Turkey and the Middle East. Tomatoes, aubergines, peppers, courgettes and onions are all used as receptacles for a delicious variety of fillings. Large leaves like vine, spinach and cabbage are stuffed with aromatic ingredients, packed in a pan and gently cooked until all the flavours are deliciously mingled.

GREEK SALAD

Anyone who has spent a holiday in Greece will have eaten a version of this salad – the Greeks' equivalent to a mixed salad. Its success relies on using the freshest of ingredients, and a good olive oil.

1 small cos lettuce, sliced
450g/1lb well-flavoured tomatoes, cut into eighths
1 cucumber, seeded and chopped
200g/7oz feta cheese, crumbled
4 spring onions, sliced
50g/2oz/½ cup black olives, stoned and halved

FOR THE DRESSING
90ml/6 tbsp good olive oil
25ml/1½ tbsp lemon juice
salt and ground black pepper

SERVES 6

1 Put all the main salad ingredients into a large bowl. Whisk together the olive oil and lemon juice, then season with salt and pepper, and pour the dressing over the salad. Mix well and serve immediately.

SPICED AUBERGINE SALAD

Serve this Middle-Eastern influenced salad with warm pitta bread as a starter or to accompany a main course rice pilaff.

2 small aubergines, sliced
75ml/5 tbsp olive oil
50ml/2fl oz/¼ cup red wine vinegar
2 garlic cloves, crushed
15ml/1 tbsp lemon juice
2.5ml/½ tsp ground cumin
2.5ml/½ tsp ground coriander
½ cucumber, thinly sliced
2 well-flavoured tomatoes, thinly sliced
30ml/2 tbsp natural yogurt
salt and ground black pepper
chopped flat leaf parsley, to garnish

SERVES 4

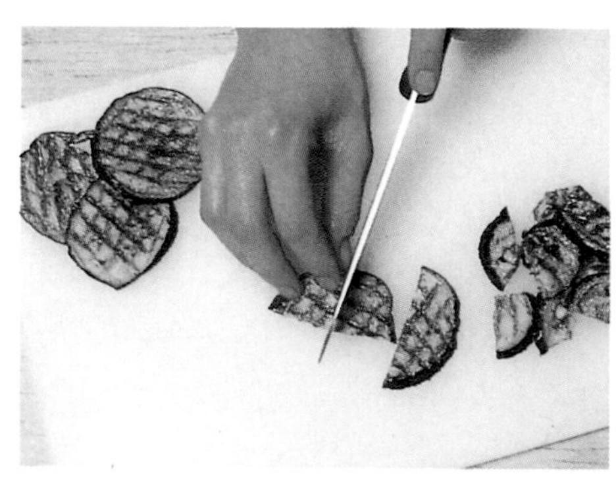

1 Preheat the grill. Brush the aubergine slices lightly with some of the oil and cook under a high heat, turning once, until golden and tender. Cut into quarters.

2 Mix together the remaining oil, vinegar, garlic, lemon juice, cumin and coriander. Season with salt and pepper and mix thoroughly. Add the warm aubergines, stir well and chill for at least 2 hours. Add the cucumber and tomatoes. Transfer to a serving dish and spoon the yogurt on top. Sprinkle with parsley.

CACIK

This refreshing yogurt dish is served all over the Eastern Mediterranean, whether as part of a mezze with marinated olives and pitta bread, or as an accompaniment to meat dishes. Greek tzatziki is very similar.

1 small cucumber
300ml/½ pint/1¼ cups thick natural yogurt
3 garlic cloves, crushed
30ml/2 tbsp chopped fresh mint
30ml/2 tbsp chopped fresh dill or parsley
salt and ground black pepper
mint or parsley and dill, to garnish
olive oil, olives and pitta bread, to serve

SERVES 6

1 Finely chop the cucumber and layer in a colander with plenty of salt. Leave for 30 minutes. Wash the cucumber in several changes of cold water and drain thoroughly. Pat dry on kitchen paper.

2 Mix together the yogurt, garlic and herbs and season with salt and pepper. Stir in the cucumber. Garnish with herbs, drizzle over a little olive oil and serve with olives and pitta bread.

BROWN BEAN SALAD

Brown beans, sometimes called "ful medames", are widely used in Egyptian cookery, and are occasionally seen in health food shops here. Dried broad beans, black or red kidney beans make a good substitute.

350g/12oz/1½ cups dried brown beans
3 thyme sprigs
2 bay leaves
1 onion, halved
4 garlic cloves, crushed
7.5ml/1½ tsp cumin seeds, crushed
3 spring onions, finely chopped
90ml/6 tbsp chopped fresh parsley
20ml/4 tsp lemon juice
90ml/6 tbsp olive oil
3 hard-boiled eggs, shelled and roughly chopped
1 pickled cucumber, roughly chopped
salt and ground black pepper

SERVES 6

1. Put the beans in a bowl with plenty of cold water and leave to soak overnight. Drain, transfer to a saucepan and cover with fresh water. Bring to the boil and boil rapidly for 10 minutes.

2. Reduce the heat and add the thyme, bay leaves and onion. Simmer very gently for about 1 hour until tender. Drain and discard the herbs and onion.

COOK'S TIP

The cooking time for dried beans can vary considerably. They may need only 45 minutes, or a lot longer.

3. Mix together the garlic, cumin, spring onions, parsley, lemon juice, oil and add a little salt and pepper. Pour over the beans and toss the ingredients lightly together.

4. Gently stir in the eggs and cucumber and serve at once.

WARM BROAD BEAN AND FETA SALAD

This recipe is loosely based on a typical medley of fresh-tasting Greek salad ingredients – broad beans, tomatoes and feta cheese. It's lovely warm or cold as a starter or main course accompaniment.

900g/2lb broad beans, shelled, or 350g/12oz shelled frozen beans
60ml/4 tbsp olive oil
175g/6oz plum tomatoes, halved, or quartered if large
4 garlic cloves, crushed
115g/4oz firm feta cheese, cut into chunks
45ml/3 tbsp chopped fresh dill
12 black olives
salt and ground black pepper
chopped fresh dill, to garnish

SERVES 4–6

1. Cook the fresh or frozen broad beans in boiling, salted water until just tender. Drain and set aside.

2. Meanwhile, heat the oil in a heavy-based frying pan and add the tomatoes and garlic. Cook until the tomatoes are beginning to colour.

3. Add the feta to the pan and toss the ingredients together for 1 minute. Mix with the drained beans, dill, olives and salt and pepper. Serve garnished with chopped dill.

HALLOUMI AND GRAPE SALAD

In Eastern Europe, firm salty halloumi cheese is often served fried for breakfast or supper. In this recipe it's tossed with sweet, juicy grapes which really complement its distinctive flavour.

FOR THE DRESSING
60ml/4 tbsp olive oil
15ml/1 tbsp lemon juice
2.5ml/½ tsp caster sugar
salt and ground black pepper
15ml/1 tbsp chopped fresh thyme or dill

FOR THE SALAD
150g/5oz mixed green salad leaves
75g/3oz seedless green grapes
75g/3oz seedless black grapes
250g/9oz halloumi cheese
45ml/3 tbsp olive oil
fresh young thyme leaves or dill, to garnish

SERVES 4

1. To make the dressing, mix together the olive oil, lemon juice and sugar. Season. Stir in the thyme or dill and set aside.

2. Toss together the salad leaves and the green and black grapes, then transfer to a large serving plate.

3. Thinly slice the cheese. Heat the oil in a large frying pan. Add the cheese and fry briefly until turning golden on the underside. Turn the cheese with a fish slice and cook the other side.

4. Arrange the cheese over the salad. Pour over the dressing and garnish with thyme or dill.

SIMPLE COOKED SALAD

A version of a popular Mediterranean recipe, this cooked salad is served as a side dish to accompany a main course. Make it the day before to enhance the flavour.

2 well-flavoured tomatoes, quartered
2 onions, chopped
½ cucumber, halved lengthways, seeded and sliced
1 green pepper, halved, seeded and chopped
30ml/2 tbsp lemon juice
45ml/3 tbsp olive oil
2 garlic cloves, crushed
30ml/2 tbsp chopped fresh coriander
salt and ground black pepper
sprigs of coriander, to garnish

SERVES 4

1 Put the tomatoes, onions, cucumber and green pepper into a pan, add 60ml/4 tbsp water and simmer for 5 minutes. Leave to cool.

2 Mix together the lemon juice, olive oil and garlic. Strain the vegetables, then transfer to a bowl. Pour over the dressing, season with salt and pepper and stir in the chopped coriander. Serve at once, garnished with coriander, if you like.

SPICY CHICK-PEA AND AUBERGINE STEW

This is a Lebanese dish, but similar recipes are found all over the Mediterranean.

3 large aubergines, cubed
200g/7oz/1 cup chick-peas, soaked overnight
60ml/4 tbsp olive oil
3 garlic cloves, chopped
2 large onions, chopped
2.5ml/½ tsp ground cumin
2.5ml/½ tsp ground cinnamon
2.5ml/½ tsp ground coriander
3 x 400g/14oz cans chopped tomatoes
salt and ground black pepper
cooked rice, to serve

FOR THE GARNISH
30ml/2 tbsp olive oil
1 onion, sliced
1 garlic clove, sliced
sprigs of coriander

SERVES 4

1 Place the aubergines in a colander and sprinkle them with salt. Sit the colander in a bowl and leave for 30 minutes, to allow the bitter juices to escape. Rinse with cold water and dry on kitchen paper.

2 Drain the chick-peas and put in a pan with enough water to cover. Bring to the boil and simmer for 30 minutes, or until tender. Drain.

3 Heat the oil in a large pan. Add the garlic and onion and cook gently, until soft. Add the spices and cook, stirring, for a few seconds. Add the aubergine and stir to coat with the spices and onion. Cook for 5 minutes. Add the tomatoes and chick-peas and season with salt and pepper. Cover and simmer for 20 minutes.

4 To make the garnish, heat the oil in a frying pan and, when very hot, add the sliced onion and garlic. Fry until golden and crisp. Serve the stew with rice, topped with the onion and garlic and garnished with coriander.

POLPETTES

Delicious little fried morsels of potato and Greek feta cheese, flavoured with dill and lemon juice.

500g/1¼lb potatoes
115g/4oz feta cheese
4 spring onions, chopped
45ml/3 tbsp chopped fresh dill
1 egg, beaten
15ml/1 tbsp lemon juice
salt and ground black pepper
flour for dredging
45ml/3 tbsp olive oil

SERVES 4

1 Boil the potatoes in their skins in lightly salted water until soft. Drain, then peel while still warm. Place in a bowl and mash. Crumble the feta cheese into the potatoes and add the spring onions, dill, egg and lemon juice and season with salt and pepper. (The cheese is salty, so taste before you add salt.) Stir well.

2 Cover the mixture and chill until firm. Divide the mixture into walnut-size balls, then flatten them slightly. Dredge with flour. Heat the oil in a frying pan and fry the polpettes until golden brown on each side. Drain on kitchen paper and serve at once.

SPICED TURNIPS WITH SPINACH AND TOMATOES

Sweet baby turnips, tender spinach and ripe tomatoes make tempting partners in this simple Eastern Mediterranean vegetable stew.

450g/1lb plum or other well-flavoured tomatoes
60ml/4 tbsp olive oil
2 onions, sliced
450g/1lb baby turnips, peeled
5ml/1 tsp paprika
2.5ml/½ tsp caster sugar
60ml/4 tbsp chopped fresh coriander
450g/1lb fresh young spinach, stalks removed
salt and ground black pepper

SERVES 6

1 Plunge the tomatoes into a bowl of boiling water for 30 seconds, then refresh in a bowl of cold water. Peel away the tomato skins and chop roughly. Heat the olive oil in a large frying pan or sauté pan and fry the onion slices for about 5 minutes until golden.

2 Add the baby turnips, tomatoes and paprika to the pan with 60ml/4 tbsp water and cook until the tomatoes are pulpy. Cover with a lid and continue cooking until the baby turnips have softened.

3 Stir in the sugar and coriander, then add the spinach and a little salt and pepper and cook for a further 2–3 minutes until the spinach has wilted. Serve warm or cold.

STUFFED TOMATOES AND PEPPERS

Colourful peppers and tomatoes make perfect containers for various meat and vegetable stuffings. This rice and herb version uses typically Greek ingredients.

VARIATION

Small aubergines or large courgettes also make good vegetables for stuffing. Halve and scoop out the centres of the vegetables, then oil the vegetable cases and bake for about 15 minutes. Chop the centres, fry for 2–3 minutes to soften and add to the stuffing mixture. Fill the aubergine or courgette cases with the stuffing and bake as for the peppers and tomatoes.

2 large ripe tomatoes
1 green pepper
1 yellow or orange pepper
60ml/4 tbsp olive oil, plus extra for sprinkling
2 onions, chopped
2 garlic cloves, crushed
50g/2oz/½ cup blanched almonds, chopped
75g/3oz/scant ½ cup long grain rice, boiled and drained
15g/½oz mint, roughly chopped
15g/½oz parsley, roughly chopped
25g/1oz/2 tbsp sultanas
45ml/3 tbsp ground almonds
salt and ground black pepper
chopped mixed herbs, to garnish

SERVES 4

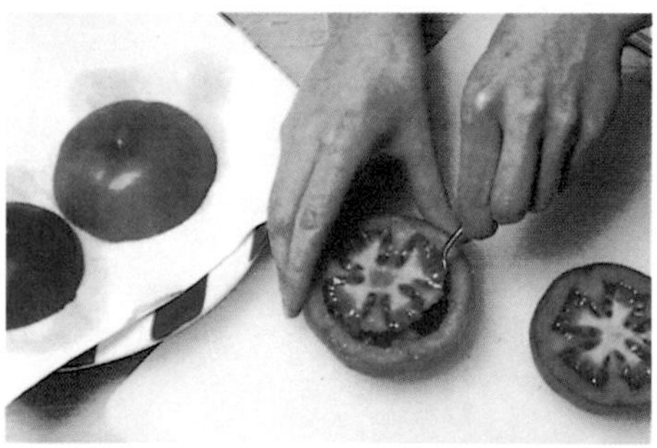

1 Preheat the oven to 190°C/375°F/Gas 5. Cut the tomatoes in half and scoop out the pulp and seeds using a teaspoon. Leave the tomatoes to drain on kitchen paper with cut sides down. Roughly chop the tomato pulp and seeds.

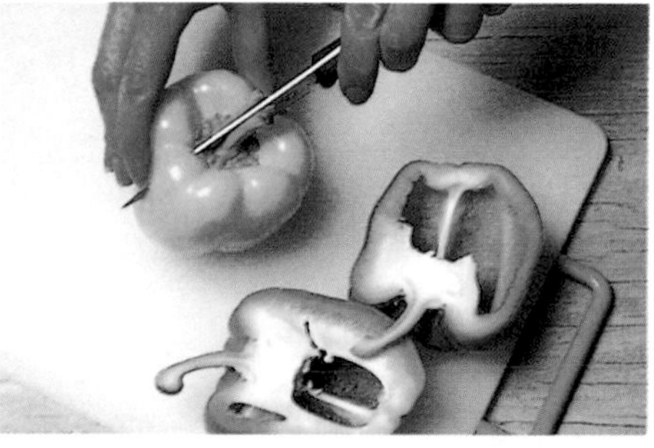

2 Halve the peppers, leaving the cores intact. Scoop out the seeds. Brush the peppers with 15ml/1 tbsp of the oil and bake on a baking tray for 15 minutes. Place the peppers and tomatoes in a shallow ovenproof dish and season with salt and pepper.

3 Fry the onions in the remaining oil for 5 minutes. Add the garlic and chopped almonds and fry for a further minute.

4 Remove the pan from the heat and stir in the rice, chopped tomatoes, mint, parsley and sultanas. Season well with salt and pepper and spoon the mixture into the tomatoes and peppers.

5 Pour 150ml/¼ pint/⅔ cup boiling water around the tomatoes and peppers and bake, uncovered, for 20 minutes. Scatter with the ground almonds and sprinkle with a little extra olive oil. Return to the oven and bake for a further 20 minutes, or until turning golden. Serve garnished with fresh herbs.

OKRA WITH CORIANDER AND TOMATOES

Okra is frequently combined with tomatoes and mild spices in various parts of the Mediterranean. Buy okra only if it is soft and velvety, not dry and shrivelled.

450g/1lb tomatoes or 400g/14oz can chopped tomatoes
450g/1lb fresh okra
45ml/3 tbsp olive oil
2 onions, thinly sliced
10ml/2 tsp coriander seeds, crushed
3 garlic cloves, crushed
2.5ml/½ tsp caster sugar
finely grated rind and juice of 1 lemon
salt and ground black pepper

SERVES 4

1 If using fresh tomatoes, plunge them into boiling water for 30 seconds, then refresh in cold water. Peel away the skins and chop.

2 Trim off any stalks from the okra and leave whole. Heat the oil in a sauté pan and fry the onions and coriander for 3–4 minutes until beginning to colour.

3 Add the okra and garlic and fry for 1 minute. Gently stir in the tomatoes and sugar and simmer gently for about 20 minutes, until the okra is tender, stirring once or twice. Stir in the lemon rind and juice and add salt and pepper to taste, adding a little more sugar if necessary. Serve warm or cold.

STUFFED PEPPERS

Couscous is a form of semolina, and is used extensively in the Middle East. It makes a good basis for a stuffing, combined with other ingredients.

6 peppers
25g/1oz/2 tbsp butter
1 onion, finely chopped
5ml/1 tsp olive oil
2.5ml/½ tsp salt
175g/6oz/1 cup couscous
25g/1oz/2 tbsp raisins
30ml/2 tbsp chopped fresh mint
1 egg yolk
salt and ground black pepper
mint leaves, to garnish

SERVES 4

1 Preheat the oven to 200°C/400°F/Gas 6. Carefully slit each pepper and remove the core and seeds. Melt the butter in a small pan and add the onion. Cook until soft.

2 To cook the couscous, bring 250ml/8fl oz/1 cup water to the boil. Add the oil and the salt, then remove the pan from the heat and add the couscous. Stir and leave to stand, covered, for 5 minutes. Stir in the cooked onion, raisins and mint, then season well with salt and pepper. Stir in the egg yolk.

3 Using a teaspoon, fill the peppers with the couscous mixture to only about three-quarters full, as the couscous will swell when cooked further. Place in a lightly oiled ovenproof dish and bake, uncovered, for about 20 minutes until tender. Serve hot or cold, garnished with the mint leaves.

STUFFED VINE LEAVES WITH GARLIC YOGURT

An old Greek recipe which comes in many guises. This meatless version is highly flavoured with fresh herbs, lemon and a little chilli.

225g/8oz packet preserved vine leaves
1 onion, finely chopped
½ bunch of spring onions, trimmed and finely chopped
60ml/4 tbsp chopped fresh parsley
10 large mint sprigs, chopped
finely grated rind of 1 lemon
2.5ml/½ tsp crushed dried chillies
7.5ml/1½ tsp fennel seeds, crushed
175g/6oz/scant 1 cup long grain rice
120ml/4fl oz/½ cup olive oil
150ml/¼ pint/⅔ cup thick natural yogurt
2 garlic cloves, crushed
salt
lemon wedges and mint leaves, to garnish (optional)

SERVES 6

1 Rinse the vine leaves in plenty of cold water. Put in a bowl, cover with boiling water and leave for 10 minutes. Drain thoroughly.

2 Mix together the onion, spring onions, parsley, mint, lemon, chilli, fennel, rice and 25ml/1½ tbsp of the olive oil. Mix thoroughly and season with salt.

3 Place a vine leaf, veined side facing upwards, on a work surface and cut off any stalk. Place a heaped teaspoonful of the rice mixture near the stalk end of the leaf.

4 Fold the stalk end of the leaf over the rice filling, then fold over the sides and carefully roll up into a neat cigar shape.

5 Repeat with the remaining filling to make about 28 stuffed leaves. If some of the vine leaves are quite small, use two and patch them together to make parcels of the same size.

6 Place any remaining leaves in the base of a large heavy-based saucepan. Pack the stuffed leaves in a single layer in the pan. Spoon over the remaining oil then add about 300ml/½ pint/1¼ cups boiling water.

COOK'S TIP

To check that the rice is cooked, lift out one stuffed leaf and cut in half. The rice should have expanded and softened to make a firm parcel. If necessary, cook the stuffed leaves a little longer, adding boiling water if the pan is becoming dry.

7 Place a small plate over the leaves to keep them submerged in the water. Cover the pan and cook on a very low heat for 45 minutes.

8 Mix together the yogurt and garlic and put in a small serving dish. Transfer the stuffed leaves to a serving plate and garnish with lemon wedges and mint, if you like. Serve with the garlic yogurt.

Fish and Seafood

The Mediterranean provides a rich source of fish, so that recipes for using the many different types are abundant. Plaki is a well-loved example, perfect for fish such as cod, grey mullet and bass, which absorb all the wonderful flavours of the other ingredients. Middle Eastern fish dishes emphasize the accompanying sauce – the choice of fish being the pick of the catch. Baked Fish with Tahini Sauce – a simple blend of tahini with olive oil and lemon juice – is classic. Squid and octopus both play an important role in Greek cookery. Squid, from the tiniest, which are lovely seared in olive oil with garlic and herbs, to huge specimens, rich with stuffings, typify Greek cookery techniques.

KING PRAWNS WITH PIQUANT TOMATO SAUCE

This spicy sauce is served with fish and seafood. Its main ingredients are sweet peppers, tomatoes, garlic and almonds.

24 raw king prawns
30–45ml/2–3 tbsp olive oil
flat leaf parsley, to garnish
lemon wedges, to serve

FOR THE SAUCE
2 well-flavoured tomatoes
60ml/4 tbsp olive oil
1 onion, chopped
4 garlic cloves, chopped
1 canned pimiento, chopped
2.5ml/½ tsp dried chilli flakes or powder
75ml/5 tbsp fish stock
30ml/2 tbsp white wine
10 blanched almonds
15ml/1 tbsp red wine vinegar
salt

SERVES 4

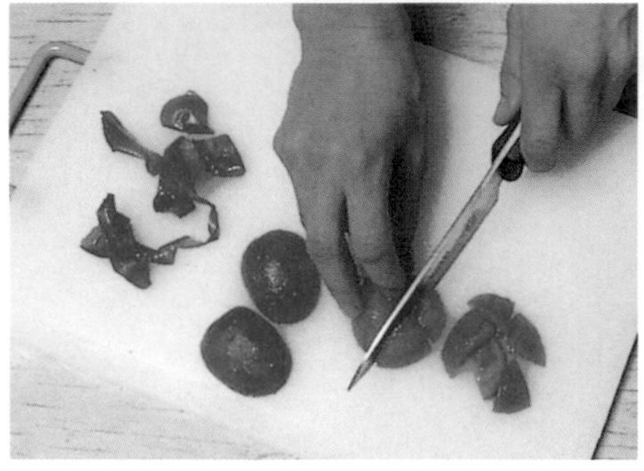

1 To make the sauce, immerse the tomatoes in boiling water for about 30 seconds, then refresh them under cold water. Peel away the skins and roughly chop the flesh.

2 Heat 30ml/2 tbsp of the oil in a pan, add the onion and 3 of the garlic cloves and cook until soft. Add the pimiento, tomatoes, chilli, fish stock and wine, then cover and simmer for 30 minutes.

3 Toast the almonds under the grill until golden. Transfer to a blender or food processor and grind coarsely. Add the remaining 30ml/2 tbsp of oil, the vinegar and the last garlic clove and process until evenly combined. Add the tomato and pimiento sauce and process until smooth. Season with salt.

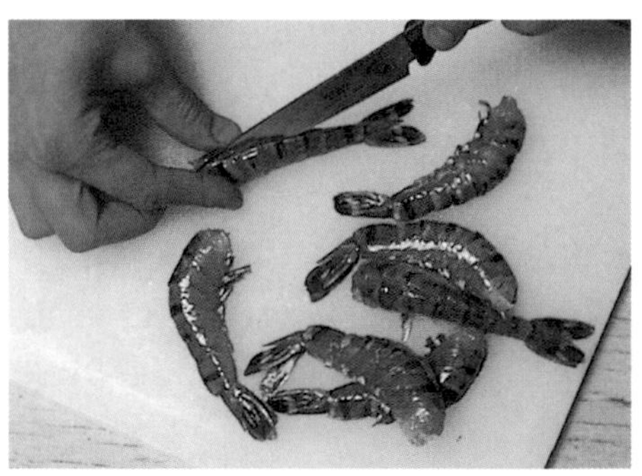

4 Remove the heads from the prawns leaving them otherwise unshelled and, with a sharp knife, slit each one down the back and remove the dark vein. Rinse and pat dry on kitchen paper. Preheat the grill. Toss the prawns in olive oil, then spread out in the grill pan. Grill for about 2–3 minutes on each side, until pink. Arrange on a serving platter with the lemon wedges, and the sauce in a small bowl. Serve at once, garnished with parsley.

GRILLED SEA BASS WITH FENNEL

This simple dish brings out the full flavour of the fish. Traditionally fennel twigs are used but, as they are hard to find, this recipe uses fennel seeds.

1 sea bass, weighing 1.75kg/4–4½lb, cleaned
60–90ml/4–6 tbsp olive oil
10–15ml/2–3 tsp fennel seeds
2 large fennel bulbs, trimmed and thinly sliced (reserve any fronds)
60ml/4 tbsp Pernod
salt and ground black pepper

SERVES 6–8

1 With a sharp knife, make three or four deep cuts in both sides of the fish. Brush the fish with olive oil and season with salt and pepper. Sprinkle the fennel seeds in the stomach cavity and in the cuts. Set aside while you cook the fennel.

2 Preheat the grill. Put the slices of fennel in a flameproof dish or on the grill rack and brush with oil. Grill for 4 minutes on each side until tender. Transfer to a large platter.

3 Place the fish on the oiled grill rack and position about 10–13cm/4–5in away from the heat. Grill for 10–12 minutes on each side, brushing with oil occasionally.

4 Transfer the fish to the platter on top of the fennel. Garnish with fennel fronds. Heat the Pernod in a small pan, light it and pour it, flaming, over the fish. Serve at once.

COD PLAKI

Greece has so much coastline, it's no wonder that fish is popular all over the country. Generally, it is treated very simply, but this recipe is a little more involved, baking the fish with onions and tomatoes.

300ml/½ pint/1¼ cups olive oil
2 onions, thinly sliced
3 large well-flavoured tomatoes, roughly chopped
3 garlic cloves, thinly sliced
5ml/1 tsp sugar
5ml/1 tsp chopped fresh dill
5ml/1 tsp chopped fresh mint
5ml/1 tsp chopped fresh celery leaves
15ml/1 tbsp chopped fresh parsley
6 cod steaks
juice of 1 lemon
salt and ground black pepper
extra dill, mint or parsley, to garnish

SERVES 6

1 Heat the oil in a large sauté pan or flameproof dish. Add the onions and cook until pale golden. Add the tomatoes, garlic, sugar, dill, mint, celery leaves and parsley with 300ml/½ pint/1¼ cups water. Season with salt and pepper, then simmer, uncovered, for 25 minutes, until the liquid has reduced by one-third.

2 Add the fish steaks and cook gently for 10–12 minutes, until the fish is just cooked. Remove from the heat and add the lemon juice (*left*). Cover and leave to stand for about 20 minutes before serving. Arrange the cod in a dish and spoon the sauce over. Garnish with herbs and serve warm or cold.

STUFFED SQUID

This Greek delicacy is best made with large squid as they are less fiddly to stuff. If you have to make do with small squid, buy about 450g/1lb.

FOR THE STUFFING
30ml/2 tbsp olive oil
1 large onion, finely chopped
2 garlic cloves, crushed
50g/2oz/1 cup fresh breadcrumbs
60ml/4 tbsp chopped fresh parsley
115g/4oz halloumi cheese, grated
salt and ground black pepper

TO FINISH
4 squid tubes, each about 18cm/7in long
900g/2lb ripe tomatoes
45ml/3 tbsp olive oil
1 large onion, chopped
5ml/1 tsp caster sugar
120ml/4fl oz/½ cup dry white wine
several rosemary sprigs
toasted pine nuts and flat leaf parsley, to garnish

SERVES 4

1 To make the stuffing, heat the oil in a frying pan and fry the onion for 3 minutes. Remove the pan from the heat and add the garlic, breadcrumbs, parsley, cheese and a little salt and pepper. Stir until thoroughly blended.

2 Dry the squid tubes on kitchen paper and fill with the prepared stuffing using a teaspoon. Secure the ends of the squid tubes with wooden cocktail sticks.

VARIATION
If you would prefer a less rich filling, halve the quantity of cheese and breadcrumbs in the stuffing and add 225g/8oz cooked spinach.

3 Plunge the tomatoes into boiling water for 30 seconds, then refresh in cold water. Peel away the skins and chop roughly.

4 Heat the oil in a frying pan or sauté pan. Add the squid and fry on all sides. Remove from the pan.

5 Add the onion to the pan and fry gently for 3 minutes. Stir in the tomatoes, sugar and wine and cook rapidly until the mixture becomes thick and pulpy.

6 Return the squid to the pan with the rosemary. Cover and cook gently for 30 minutes. Slice the squid and serve on individual plates with the sauce. Scatter over the pine nuts and garnish with parsley.

PAN-FRIED RED MULLET WITH BASIL AND CITRUS

Red mullet is popular all over the Mediterranean. This recipe combines it with oranges and lemons, which grow in abundance.

4 red mullet, about 225g/8oz each, filleted
90ml/6 tbsp olive oil
10 peppercorns, crushed
2 oranges, one peeled and sliced and one squeezed
1 lemon
30ml/2 tbsp plain flour
15g/½oz/1 tbsp butter
2 drained canned anchovies, chopped
60ml/4 tbsp shredded fresh basil
salt and ground black pepper

SERVES 4

1 Place the fish fillets in a shallow dish in a single layer. Pour over the olive oil and sprinkle with the crushed peppercorns. Lay the orange slices on top of the fish. Cover the dish, and leave to marinate in the fridge for at least 4 hours.

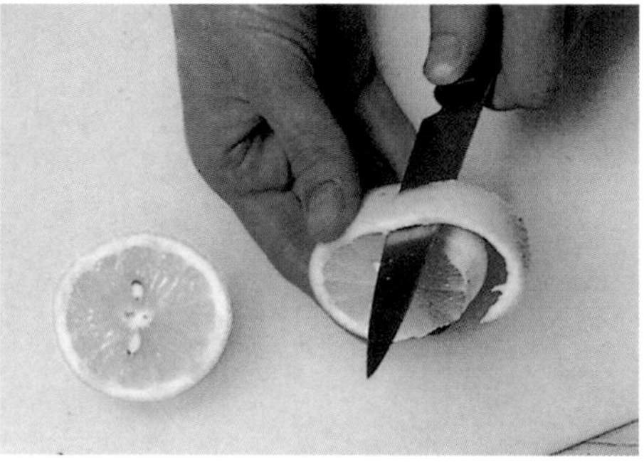

2 Halve the lemon. Remove the skin and pith from one half using a small sharp knife, and slice thinly. Squeeze the juice from the other half.

COOK'S TIP

If you prefer, use other fish fillets for this dish, such as lemon sole, haddock or hake.

3 Lift the fish out of the marinade, and pat dry on kitchen paper. Reserve the marinade and orange slices. Season the fish with salt and pepper and dust lightly with flour.

4 Heat 45ml/3 tbsp of the marinade in a frying pan. Add the fish and fry for 2 minutes on each side. Remove from the pan and keep warm. Discard the marinade that is left in the pan.

5 Melt the butter in the pan with any of the remaining original marinade. Add the anchovies and cook until completely softened.

6 Stir in the orange and lemon juice, then check the seasoning and simmer until slightly reduced. Stir in the basil. Pour the sauce over the fish and garnish with the reserved orange slices and the lemon slices.

OCTOPUS AND RED WINE STEW

Unless you're happy to clean and prepare octopus for this Greek dish, buy one that's ready for cooking.

900g/2lb prepared octopus
450g/1lb onions, sliced
2 bay leaves
450g/1lb ripe tomatoes
60ml/4 tbsp olive oil
4 garlic cloves, crushed
5ml/1 tsp caster sugar
15ml/1 tbsp chopped fresh oregano or rosemary
30ml/2 tbsp chopped fresh parsley
150ml/¼ pint/⅔ cup red wine
30ml/2 tbsp red wine vinegar
chopped fresh herbs, to garnish
warm bread and pine nuts, to serve

SERVES 4

1 Put the octopus in a saucepan of gently simmering water with a quarter of the onions and the bay leaves. Cook gently for 1 hour.

2 While the octopus is cooking, plunge the tomatoes into boiling water for 30 seconds, then refresh in cold water. Peel away the skins and chop roughly.

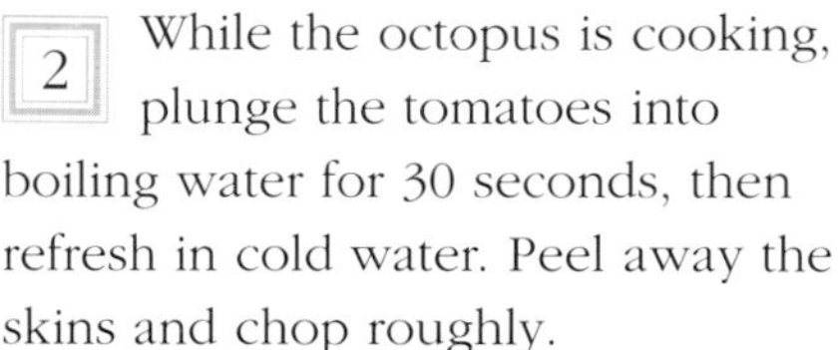

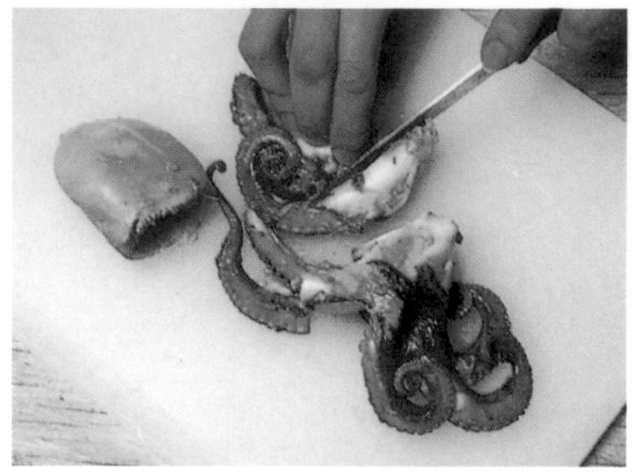

3 Drain the octopus and, using a sharp knife, cut it into bite-size pieces. Discard the head.

4 Heat the oil in a saucepan and fry the octopus, the remaining onions and the garlic for 3 minutes. Add the tomatoes, sugar, oregano or rosemary, parsley, wine and vinegar and cook, stirring, for 5 minutes until pulpy.

5 Cover the pan and cook over the lowest possible heat for about 1½ hours until the sauce is thickened and the octopus is tender. Garnish with fresh herbs and serve with plenty of warm bread, and pine nuts to scatter on top.

FRESH TUNA AND TOMATO STEW

A deliciously simple dish that relies on good basic ingredients. Serve with plain boiled rice and a green vegetable.

12 baby onions, peeled
900g/2lb ripe tomatoes
675g/1½lb fresh tuna
45ml/3 tbsp olive oil
2 garlic cloves, crushed
45ml/3 tbsp chopped fresh herbs
2 bay leaves
2.5ml/½ tsp caster sugar
30ml/2 tbsp sun-dried tomato paste
150ml/¼ pint/⅔ cup dry white wine
salt and ground black pepper
baby courgettes and fresh herbs, to garnish

SERVES 4

VARIATION

Two large mackerel make a more readily available alternative to the tuna. Fillet them and cut into chunks or simply lay the whole fish over the sauce and cook, covered with a lid until the mackerel is cooked through. Sage, rosemary or oregano all go extremely well with this dish. Choose whichever you prefer, or use a mixture of one or two.

1 Leave the onions whole and cook in a pan of boiling water for 4–5 minutes until softened. Drain.

2 Plunge the tomatoes into boiling water for 30 seconds, then refresh in cold water. Peel away the skins and chop roughly.

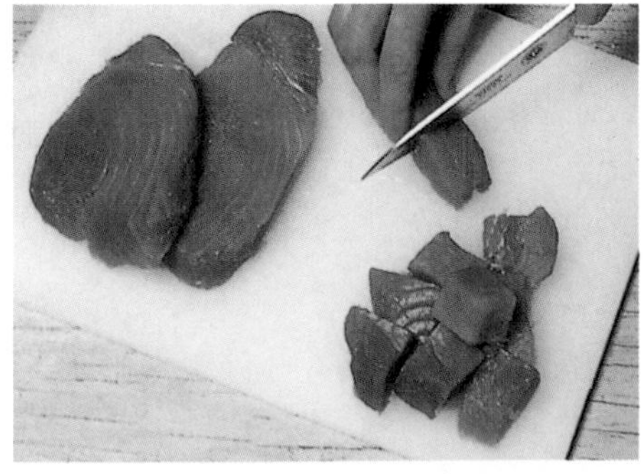

3 Cut the tuna into 2.5cm/1in chunks. Heat the oil in a large frying or sauté pan and quickly fry the tuna until browned. Drain.

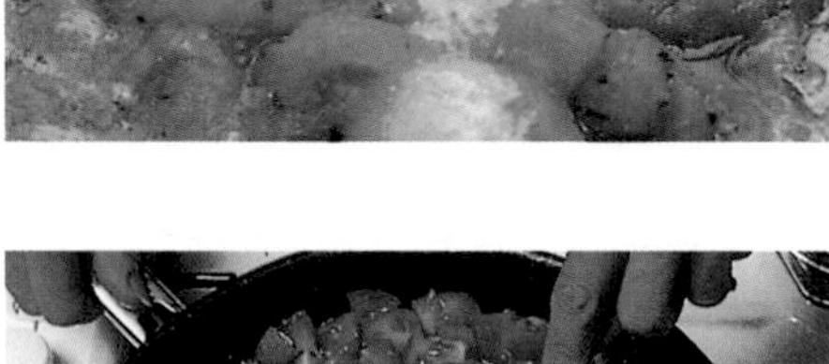

4 Add the onions, garlic, tomatoes, chopped herbs, bay leaves, sugar, tomato paste and wine and bring to the boil, breaking up the tomatoes with a wooden spoon.

5 Reduce the heat and simmer gently for 5 minutes. Return the fish to the pan and cook for a further 5 minutes. Season, and serve hot, garnished with baby courgettes and fresh herbs.

BAKED FISH WITH TAHINI SAUCE

This recipe evokes all the colour and rich flavours of Eastern Mediterranean cuisine. Choose any whole white fish, such as sea bass, hake, bream or snapper.

1 whole fish, about 1.1kg/2½lb, scaled and cleaned
10ml/2 tsp coriander seeds
4 garlic cloves, sliced
10ml/2 tsp harissa sauce
90ml/6 tbsp olive oil
6 plum tomatoes, sliced
1 mild onion, sliced
3 preserved lemons or 1 fresh lemon
plenty of fresh herbs, such as bay leaves, thyme and rosemary
salt and ground black pepper

FOR THE SAUCE
75ml/3fl oz/⅓ cup light tahini
juice of 1 lemon
1 garlic clove, crushed
45ml/3 tbsp finely chopped fresh parsley or coriander
extra herbs, to garnish

SERVES 4

1 Preheat the oven to 200°C/400°F/Gas 6. Grease the base and sides of a large shallow ovenproof dish or roasting tin.

2 Slash the fish diagonally on both sides with a sharp knife. Finely crush the coriander seeds and garlic with a pestle and mortar. Mix with the harissa sauce and about 60ml/4 tbsp of the olive oil.

3 Spread a little of the harissa, coriander and garlic paste inside the cavity of the fish. Spread the remainder over each side of the fish and set aside.

4 Scatter the tomatoes, onion and preserved or fresh lemon into the dish. (Thinly slice the lemon if using fresh.) Sprinkle with the remaining oil and season with salt and pepper. Lay the fish on top and tuck plenty of herbs around it.

5 Bake, uncovered, for about 25 minutes, or until the fish has turned opaque – test by piercing the thickest part with a knife.

6 Meanwhile, make the sauce. Put the tahini, lemon juice, garlic and parsley or coriander in a small saucepan with 120ml/4fl oz/½ cup water and add a little salt and pepper. Cook gently until smooth and heated through. Serve in a separate dish.

COOK'S TIP

If you can't get a suitable large fish, use small whole fish such as red mullet or even cod or haddock steaks. Remember to reduce the cooking time slightly.

Poultry and Meat

Since meat is scarcer than fish in the countries of the Eastern Mediterranean, the traditional recipes are designed to make a little go a long way, as in the classic Greek Moussaka, for which minced lamb is layered with aubergines, then topped with cheese sauce and in Lamb Pilau, where rice gives substance to the dish. Spices, nuts and dried fruits are often mixed with the meat to make delicious fillings for little parcels of filo, such as Chicken and Apricot Filo Pie. These versatile dishes are great when entertaining a large group of friends.

DUCK BREASTS WITH A WALNUT AND POMEGRANATE SAUCE

This is an extremely exotic sweet and sour dish which originally came from Persia.

60ml/4 tbsp olive oil
2 onions, very thinly sliced
2.5ml/½ tsp ground turmeric
400g/14oz/3½ cups walnuts, roughly chopped
1 litre/1¾ pints/4 cups duck or chicken stock
6 pomegranates
30ml/2 tbsp caster sugar
60ml/4 tbsp lemon juice
4 duck breasts, about 225g/8oz each
salt and ground black pepper

COOK'S TIP

Choose pomegranates with shiny, brightly coloured skins. The juice stains, so take care when cutting them. Only the seeds are used in cooking, the pith is discarded.

1 Heat half the oil in a frying pan. Add the onions and turmeric, and cook gently until soft. Transfer to a pan, add the walnuts and stock, then season with salt and pepper. Stir, then bring to the boil and simmer the mixture, uncovered, for 20 minutes.

2 Cut the pomegranates in half and scoop out the seeds into a bowl. Reserve the seeds of one pomegranate. Transfer the remaining seeds to a blender or food processor, and process to break them up. Strain through a sieve, to extract the juice, and stir in the sugar and lemon juice.

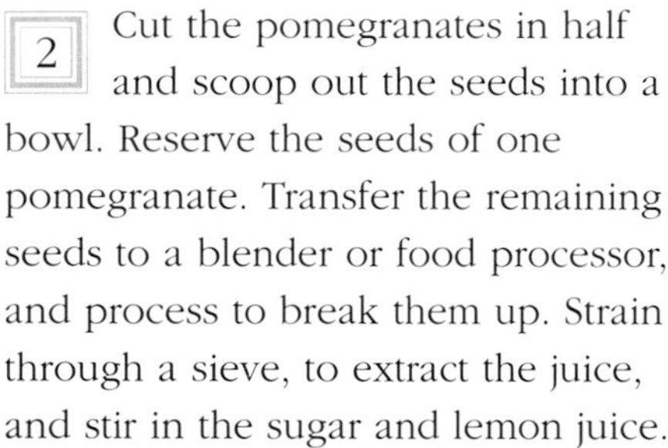

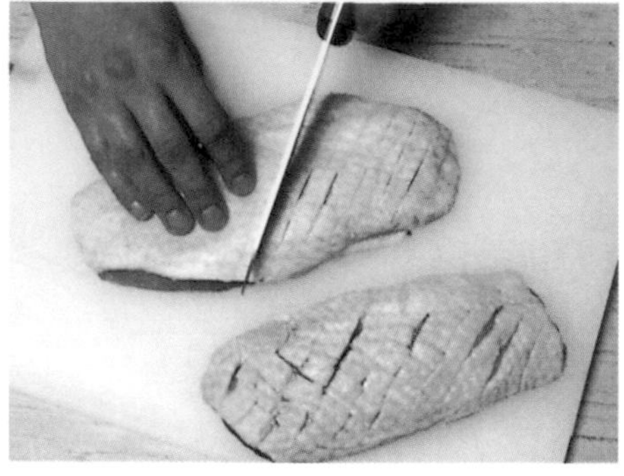

3 Score the skin of the duck breasts in a lattice fashion with a sharp knife. Heat the remaining oil in a frying pan or char grill and place the duck breasts in it, skin side down.

4 Cook gently for 10 minutes, pouring off the fat from time to time, until the skin is dark golden and crisp. Turn them over and cook for a further 3–4 minutes. Transfer to a plate and leave to rest.

5 Deglaze the frying pan or char grill with the pomegranate juice mixture, stirring with a wooden spoon, then add the walnut and stock mixture and simmer for 15 minutes until the sauce has thickened slightly. Serve the duck breasts sliced, drizzled with a little sauce, and garnished with the reserved pomegranate seeds. Serve the remaining sauce separately.

CIRCASSIAN CHICKEN

This is a Turkish dish, which is popular all over the Middle East. The chicken is poached and served cold with a flavoursome walnut sauce.

1.5kg/3–3½ lb chicken
2 onions, quartered
1 carrot, sliced
1 celery stick, trimmed and sliced
6 peppercorns
3 slices bread, crusts removed
2 garlic cloves, roughly chopped
400g/14oz/3½ cups chopped walnuts
15ml/1 tbsp walnut oil
salt and ground black pepper
chopped walnuts and paprika, to garnish

SERVES 6

1. Place the chicken in a large pan, with the onions, carrot, celery and peppercorns. Add enough water to cover, and bring to the boil. Simmer for about 1 hour, uncovered, until the chicken is tender. Leave to cool in the stock. Drain the chicken, reserving the stock.

2. Tear up the bread and soak in 90ml/6 tbsp of the chicken stock. Transfer to a blender or food processor, with the garlic and walnuts, and add 250ml/8fl oz/1 cup of the remaining stock. Process until smooth, then transfer to a pan.

3. Over a low heat, gradually add more chicken stock to the sauce, stirring constantly, until it is of a thick pouring consistency. Season with salt and pepper, remove from the heat and leave to cool in the pan. Skin and bone the chicken, and cut into bite-size chunks.

4. Place in a bowl and add a little of the sauce. Stir to coat the chicken, then arrange on a serving dish. Spoon the remaining sauce over the chicken, and drizzle with the walnut oil. Sprinkle with walnuts and paprika and serve at once.

CHICKEN WITH LEMONS AND OLIVES

Preserved lemons and limes are frequently used in Mediterranean cookery. They have a gentle flavour which can enhance all kinds of meat and fish dishes.

2.5ml/½ tsp ground cinnamon
2.5ml/½ tsp ground turmeric
1.5kg/3–3½lb chicken
30ml/2 tbsp olive oil
1 large onion, thinly sliced
5cm/2in piece fresh root ginger, grated
600ml/1 pint/2½ cups chicken stock
2 preserved lemons or limes, or fresh, cut into wedges
75g/3oz/½ cup pitted brown olives
15ml/1 tbsp clear honey
60ml/4 tbsp chopped fresh coriander
salt and ground black pepper
coriander sprigs, to garnish

SERVES 4

1 Preheat the oven to 190°C/375°F/Gas 5. Mix the ground cinnamon and turmeric in a bowl with a little salt and pepper and rub all over the chicken skin to give an even coating.

2 Heat the oil in a large sauté or shallow frying pan and fry the chicken on all sides until it turns golden. Transfer the chicken to an ovenproof dish.

3 Add the sliced onion to the pan and fry for 3 minutes. Stir in the grated ginger and the chicken stock and bring just to the boil. Pour over the chicken, cover with a lid and bake in the oven for 30 minutes.

4 Remove the chicken from the oven and add the lemons or limes, brown olives and honey. Bake, uncovered, for a further 45 minutes until the chicken is tender.

5 Stir in the coriander and season to taste. Garnish with coriander sprigs and serve at once.

CHICKEN AND APRICOT FILO PIE

The filling for this pie has a Middle Eastern flavour – minced chicken combined with apricots, bulgur wheat, nuts and spices.

75g/3oz/½ cup bulgur wheat
75g/3oz/6 tbsp butter
1 onion, chopped
450g/1lb minced chicken
50g/2oz/¼ cup ready-to-eat dried apricots, finely chopped
25g/1oz/¼ cup blanched almonds, chopped
5ml/1 tsp ground cinnamon
2.5ml/½ tsp ground allspice
50ml/2fl oz/¼ cup Greek yogurt
15ml/1 tbsp snipped fresh chives
30ml/2 tbsp chopped fresh parsley
6 large sheets filo pastry
salt and ground black pepper
chives, to garnish

SERVES 6

1 Preheat the oven to 200°C/400°F/Gas 6. Put the bulgur wheat in a bowl with 120ml/4fl oz/½ cup boiling water. Soak for 5–10 minutes, until the water is absorbed.

2 Heat 25g/1oz/2 tbsp of the butter in a pan, and gently fry the onion and chicken until pale golden.

3 Stir in the apricots, almonds and bulgur wheat and cook for a further 2 minutes. Remove from the heat and stir in the cinnamon, allspice, yogurt, chives and parsley. Season to taste with salt and pepper.

4 Melt the remaining butter. Unroll the filo pastry and cut into 25cm/10in rounds. Keep the pastry rounds covered with a clean, damp dish towel to prevent drying.

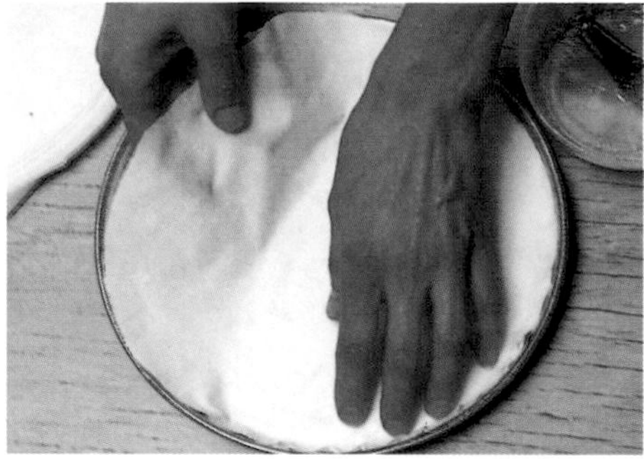

5 Line a 23cm/9in loose-based flan tin with three of the pastry rounds, brushing each one with butter as you layer them. Spoon in the chicken mixture, cover with three more pastry rounds, brushed with melted butter as before.

6 Crumple the remaining rounds and place them on top of the pie, then brush over any remaining melted butter. Bake the pie for about 30 minutes, until the pastry is golden brown and crisp. Serve Chicken and Apricot Filo Pie hot or cold, cut in wedges and garnished with chives.

AFELIA

This lightly-spiced pork stew makes a really delicious supper dish served simply, as it would be in Cyprus, with warmed bread, a leafy salad and a few olives.

675g/1½lb pork fillet, boneless leg or chump steaks
20ml/4 tsp coriander seeds
2.5ml/½ tsp caster sugar
45ml/3 tbsp olive oil
2 large onions, sliced
300ml/½ pint/1¼ cups red wine
salt and ground black pepper
fresh coriander, to garnish

SERVES 4

COOK'S TIP
A coffee grinder can also be used to grind the coriander seeds. Alternatively, use 15ml/1 tbsp ground coriander.

1 Cut the pork into small chunks, discarding any excess fat. Crush the coriander seeds with a pestle and mortar until fairly finely ground.

2 Mix the coriander seeds with the sugar and salt and pepper and rub all over the meat. Leave to marinate for up to 4 hours.

3 Preheat the oven to 160°C/325°F/Gas 3. Heat 30ml/2 tbsp of the oil in a frying pan over a high heat. Brown the meat quickly, then transfer to an ovenproof dish.

4 Add the remaining oil to the pan and fry the onions until beginning to colour. Stir in the wine and a little salt and pepper and bring just to the boil.

5 Pour the onion and wine mixture over the meat and cover with a lid. Bake for 1 hour, or until the meat is very tender. Serve scattered with fresh coriander.

LAMB PILAU

Here we have a delicious combination of rice, lamb, spices, nuts and fruit – a typical Middle Eastern dish.

40g/1½oz/3 tbsp butter
1 large onion, finely chopped
450g/1lb lamb fillet, cut into small cubes
2.5ml/½ tsp ground cinnamon
30ml/2 tbsp tomato purée
45ml/3 tbsp chopped fresh parsley
115g/4oz/½ cup ready-to-eat dried apricots, halved
75g/3oz/¾ cup pistachio nuts
450g/1lb long grain rice, rinsed
salt and ground black pepper
flat leaf parsley, to garnish

SERVES 4

1 Heat the butter in a large heavy-based pan. Add the onion and cook until soft and golden. Add the cubed lamb and brown on all sides. Add the cinnamon and season with salt and pepper. Cover and cook gently for 10 minutes.

2 Add the tomato purée and enough water to cover the meat. Stir in the parsley, bring to the boil, cover and simmer very gently for 1½ hours, until the meat is tender. Chop the pistachio nuts.

3 Add enough water to the pan to make up to about 600ml/1 pint/2½ cups liquid. Add the apricots, pistachio nuts and rice, bring to the boil, cover tightly and simmer for about 20 minutes, until the rice is cooked. (You may need to add a little more water, if necessary.) Transfer to a warmed serving dish and garnish with parsley before serving.

GREEK LAMB SAUSAGES WITH TOMATO SAUCE

The Greek name for these sausages is soudzoukakia. They are more like elongated meatballs than the type of sausage we are accustomed to. Passata is sieved tomato, which can be bought in cartons or jars.

50g/2oz/1 cup fresh breadcrumbs
150ml/¼ pint/⅔ cup milk
675g/1½lb minced lamb
30ml/2 tbsp grated onion
3 garlic cloves, crushed
10ml/2 tsp ground cumin
30ml/2 tbsp chopped fresh parsley
flour for dusting
olive oil for frying
600ml/1 pint/2½ cups passata
5ml/1 tsp sugar
2 bay leaves
1 small onion, peeled
salt and ground black pepper
flat leaf parsley, to garnish

SERVES 4

1 Mix together the breadcrumbs and milk. Add the lamb, onion, garlic, cumin and parsley and season with salt and pepper.

2 Shape the mixture with your hands into little fat sausages, about 5cm/2in long and roll them in flour. Heat about 60ml/4 tbsp olive oil in a frying pan.

3 Fry the sausages for about 8 minutes, turning them until evenly browned. Remove and place on kitchen paper to drain.

4 Put the passata, sugar, bay leaves and whole onion in a pan and simmer for 20 minutes. Add the sausages and cook for 10 minutes more. Serve garnished with parsley.

MOUSSAKA

Like many popular classics, a real moussaka bears little resemblance to the imitations experienced in many Greek tourist resorts. This one is mildly spiced, moist but not dripping in grease, and encased in a golden baked crust.

900g/2lb aubergines
120ml/4fl oz/½ cup olive oil
2 large tomatoes
2 large onions, sliced
450g/1lb minced lamb
1.5ml/¼ tsp ground cinnamon
1.5ml/¼ tsp ground allspice
30ml/2 tbsp tomato purée
45ml/3 tbsp chopped fresh parsley
120ml/4fl oz/½ cup dry white wine
salt and ground black pepper

FOR THE SAUCE
50g/2oz/4 tbsp butter
50g/2oz/½ cup plain flour
600ml/1 pint/2½ cups milk
1.5ml/¼ tsp grated nutmeg
25g/1oz/⅓ cup grated Parmesan cheese
45ml/3 tbsp toasted breadcrumbs

SERVES 6

1 Cut the aubergines into 5mm/¼in thick slices. Layer the slices in a colander, sprinkling each layer with plenty of salt. Leave to stand for 30 minutes.

2 Rinse the aubergines in several changes of cold water. Squeeze gently with your fingers to remove the excess water, then pat them dry on kitchen paper.

3 Heat some of the oil in a large frying pan. Fry the aubergine slices in batches until golden on both sides, adding more oil when necessary. Leave the fried aubergine slices to drain on kitchen paper.

4 Plunge the tomatoes into boiling water for 30 seconds, then refresh in cold water. Peel away the skins and chop roughly.

5 Preheat the oven to 180°C/350°F/Gas 4. Heat 30ml/2 tbsp oil in a saucepan. Add the onions and lamb and fry gently for 5 minutes, stirring and breaking up the lamb with a wooden spoon.

VARIATION

Sliced and sautéed courgettes or potatoes can be used instead of the aubergines in this dish.

6 Add the tomatoes, cinnamon, allspice, tomato purée, parsley, wine and pepper and bring to the boil. Reduce the heat, cover with a lid and simmer gently for 15 minutes.

7 Spoon alternate layers of the aubergines and meat mixture into a shallow ovenproof dish, finishing with a layer of aubergines.

8 To make the sauce, melt the butter in a small pan and stir in the flour. Cook, stirring, for 1 minute. Remove from the heat and gradually blend in the milk. Return to the heat and cook, stirring, for 2 minutes, until thickened. Add the nutmeg, cheese and salt and pepper. Pour the sauce over the aubergines and sprinkle with the breadcrumbs. Bake for 45 minutes until golden. Serve hot, sprinkled with extra black pepper, if you like.

KLEFTIKO

For this Greek recipe, marinated lamb steaks or chops are slow-cooked to develop an unbeatable, meltingly tender flavour. The dish is sealed, like a pie, with a flour dough lid to trap succulence and flavour, although a tight-fitting foil cover, if less attractive, will serve equally well.

juice of 1 lemon
15ml/1 tbsp chopped fresh oregano
4 lamb leg steaks or chump chops with bones
30ml/2 tbsp olive oil
2 large onions, thinly sliced
2 bay leaves
150ml/¼ pint/⅔ cup dry white wine
225g/8oz/2 cups plain flour
salt and ground black pepper

SERVES 4

COOK'S TIP

They are not absolutely essential for this dish, but lamb steaks or chops with bones will provide lots of additional flavour. Boiled potatoes make a delicious accompaniment.

1 Mix together the lemon juice, oregano and salt and pepper, and brush over both sides of the lamb steaks or chops. Leave to marinate for at least 4 hours or overnight.

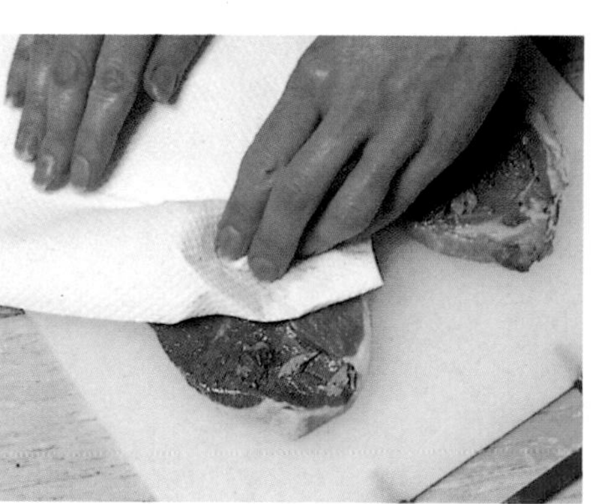

2 Preheat the oven to 160°C/325°F/Gas 3. Drain the lamb, reserving the marinade, and dry the lamb with kitchen paper. Heat the olive oil in a large frying pan or sauté pan and fry the lamb over a high heat until browned on both sides.

3 Transfer the lamb to a shallow pie dish. Scatter the sliced onions and bay leaves around the lamb, then pour over the white wine and the reserved marinade.

4 Mix the flour with sufficient water to make a firm dough. Moisten the rim of the pie dish. Roll out the dough on a floured surface and use to cover the dish so that it is tightly sealed.

5 Bake for 2 hours, then break away the dough crust and serve the lamb hot with boiled potatoes.

HUMMUS BI TAHINA

Blending chick-peas with garlic and oil makes a surprisingly creamy purée that is delicious as part of a Turkish-style mezze, or as a dip with vegetables. Leftovers make a good sandwich filler.

150g/5oz/¾ cup dried chick-peas
juice of 2 lemons
2 garlic cloves, sliced
30ml/2 tbsp olive oil
pinch of cayenne pepper
150ml/¼ pint/⅔ cup tahini paste
salt and ground black pepper
extra olive oil and cayenne pepper for sprinkling
flat leaf parsley, to garnish

SERVES 4–6

1. Put the chick-peas in a bowl with plenty of cold water and leave to soak overnight.

2. Drain the chick-peas and cover with fresh water in a saucepan. Bring to the boil and boil rapidly for 10 minutes. Reduce the heat and simmer gently for about 1 hour until soft. Drain.

3. Process the chick-peas in a food processor to a smooth purée. Add the lemon juice, garlic, olive oil, cayenne pepper and tahini and blend until creamy, scraping the mixture down from the sides of the bowl.

4. Season the purée with salt and pepper and transfer to a serving dish. Sprinkle with oil and cayenne pepper and serve garnished with a few parsley sprigs.

COOK'S TIP

For convenience, canned chick-peas can be used instead. Allow two 400g/14oz cans and drain them thoroughly. Tahini paste can now be purchased from most supermarkets or health food shops.

SPICED RICE AND LENTILS

Lentils are cooked with spices in many ways in the Middle East and two important staples come together in this dish, which can be served hot or cold.

350g/12oz/1½ cups large brown lentils, soaked overnight in water
2 large onions
45ml/3 tbsp olive oil
15ml/1 tbsp ground cumin
2.5ml/½ tsp ground cinnamon
225g/8oz/generous 1 cup long grain rice
salt and ground black pepper
flat leaf parsley, to garnish

SERVES 6

1 Drain the lentils and put in a large pan. Add enough water to cover by 5cm/2in. Bring to the boil, cover and simmer for 40 minutes to 1½ hours, or until tender. Drain thoroughly.

2 Finely chop one onion, and slice the other. Heat 15ml/1 tbsp oil in a pan, add the chopped onion and fry until soft. Add the lentils, salt, pepper, cumin and cinnamon.

3 Measure the volume of rice and add it, with the same volume of water, to the lentil mixture. Cover and simmer for about 20 minutes, until both the rice and lentils are tender. Heat the remaining oil in a frying pan, and cook the sliced onion until very dark brown. Tip the rice mixture into a serving bowl, sprinkle with the onion and serve hot or cold, garnished with flat leaf parsley.

OLIVE BREAD

Olive breads are popular all over the Mediterranean. For this Greek recipe use rich oily olives or those marinated in herbs rather than canned ones.

2 red onions, thinly sliced
30ml/2 tbsp olive oil
225g/8oz/1⅓ cups pitted black or green olives
750g/1¾lb/7 cups strong plain flour
7.5ml/1½ tsp salt
20ml/4 tsp easy-blend dried yeast
45ml/3 tbsp each roughly chopped parsley, coriander or mint

MAKES TWO 675G/1½LB LOAVES

1 Fry the onions in the oil until soft. Roughly chop the olives.

2 Put the flour, salt, yeast and parsley, coriander or mint in a large bowl with the olives and fried onions and pour in 475ml/16fl oz/2 cups hand-hot water.

VARIATION

Shape the dough into 16 small rolls. Slash the tops as above and reduce the cooking time to 25 minutes.

3 Mix to a dough using a round-bladed knife, adding a little more water if the mixture feels dry.

4 Turn out on to a lightly floured surface and knead for about 10 minutes. Put in a clean bowl, cover with clear film and leave in a warm place until doubled in bulk.

5 Preheat the oven to 220°C/425°F/Gas 7. Lightly grease two baking sheets. Turn the dough on to a floured surface and cut in half. Shape into two rounds and place on the baking sheets. Cover loosely with lightly oiled clear film and leave until doubled in size.

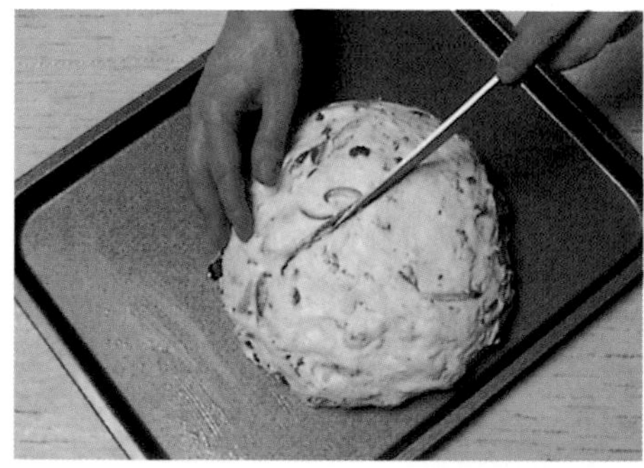

6 Slash the tops of the loaves with a knife then bake for about 40 minutes or until the loaves sound hollow when tapped on the bottom. Transfer to a wire rack to cool.

GREEK EASTER BREAD

In Greece, Easter celebrations are very important, and involve much preparation in the kitchen. This bread is sold in all the bakers' shops, and also made at home. It is traditionally decorated with red dyed eggs.

25g/1oz fresh yeast
120ml/4fl oz/½ cup warm milk
675g/1½lb /6 cups strong plain flour
2 eggs, beaten
2.5ml/½ tsp caraway seeds
15ml/1 tbsp caster sugar
15ml/1 tbsp brandy
50g/2oz/4 tbsp butter, melted
1 egg white, beaten
2–3 hard-boiled eggs, dyed red
50g/2oz/½ cup split almonds

MAKES 1 LOAF

1 Crumble the yeast into a bowl. Mix with one or two tablespoons of warm water, until softened. Add the milk and 115g/4oz/1 cup of the flour and mix to a creamy consistency. Cover with a cloth, and leave in a warm place to rise for 1 hour.

COOK'S TIP

You can often buy fresh yeast from bakers' shops. It should be pale cream in colour with a firm but crumbly texture.

2 Sift the remaining flour into a large bowl and make a well in the centre. Pour the risen yeast into the well, and draw in a little of the flour from the sides. Add the eggs, caraway seeds, sugar, and brandy. Incorporate the remaining flour, until the mixture begins to form a dough.

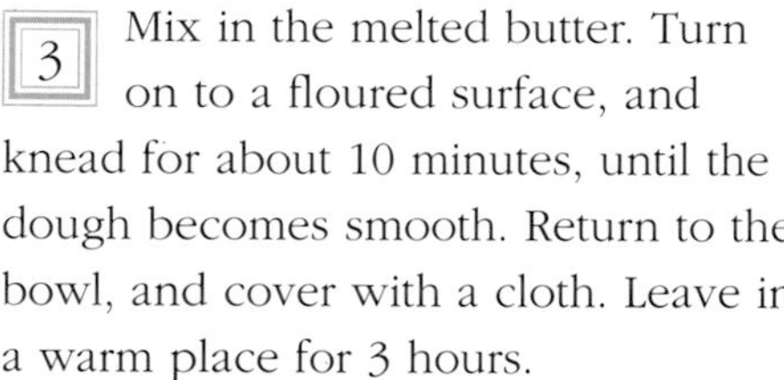

3 Mix in the melted butter. Turn on to a floured surface, and knead for about 10 minutes, until the dough becomes smooth. Return to the bowl, and cover with a cloth. Leave in a warm place for 3 hours.

4 Preheat the oven to 180°C/350°F/Gas 4. Knock back the dough, turn on to a floured surface and knead for a minute or two. Divide the dough into three, and roll each piece into a long sausage. Make a plait as shown above, and place the loaf on a greased baking sheet.

5 Tuck the ends under, brush with the egg white and decorate with the eggs and split almonds. Bake for about 1 hour, until the loaf sounds hollow when tapped on the bottom. Cool on a wire rack.

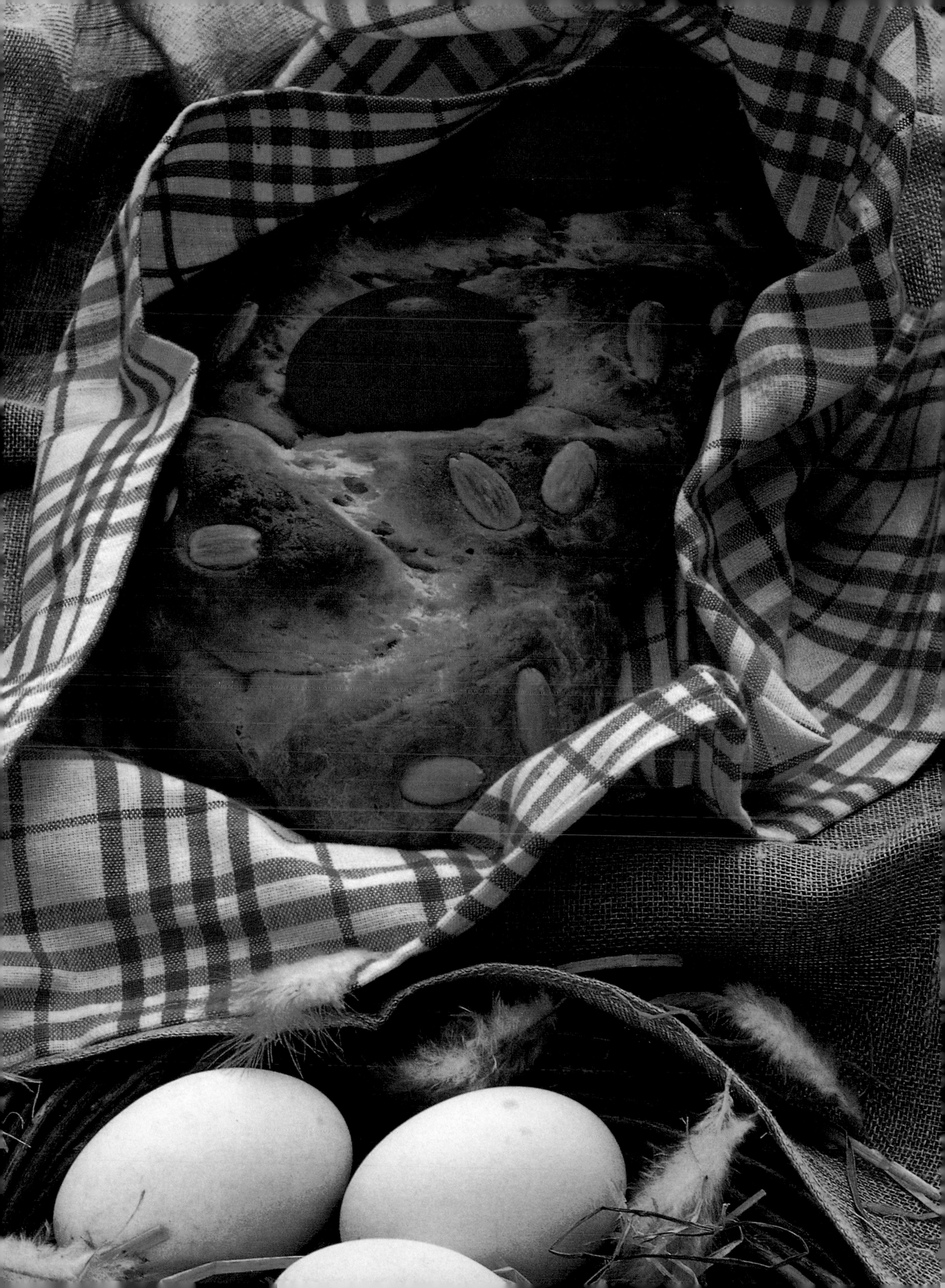

Desserts and Pastries

Desserts take full advantage of the marvellous fresh fruit and nuts of Greece and the Eastern Mediterranean, while honey, which is also abundantly produced, is the preferred sweetener, as in the recipes for Fresh Figs with Honey and Wine, and Honey and Pine Nut Tart. In Greece, Turkey, Lebanon and Egypt small sweet pastries and sweetmeats are enjoyed as a between-meal snack with good strong coffee. Served in small pieces, they make a wonderful contrast to the bitterness of the coffee. Semolina and Nut Halva is a light version of a syrup-steeped cake that is perfect either with coffee or as a dessert with cream.

FRESH FIGS WITH HONEY AND WINE

Any variety of figs can be used in this recipe, their ripeness determining the cooking time. Choose ones that are plump and firm, and use quickly as they don't store well.

450ml/¾ pint/1⅞ cups dry white wine
75g/3oz/⅓ cup clear honey
50g/2oz/¼ cup caster sugar
1 small orange
8 whole cloves
450g/1lb fresh figs
1 cinnamon stick
mint sprigs, or bay leaves, to decorate

FOR THE CREAM
300ml/½ pint/1¼ cups double cream
1 vanilla pod
5ml/1 tsp caster sugar

SERVES 6

1 Put the wine, honey and sugar in a heavy-based saucepan and heat gently until the sugar dissolves.

2 Stud the orange with the cloves and add to the syrup with the figs and cinnamon. Cover and simmer very gently for 5–10 minutes until the figs are softened. Transfer to a serving dish and leave to cool.

3 Put 150ml/¼ pint/⅔ cup of the cream in a small saucepan with the vanilla pod. Bring almost to the boil, then leave to cool and infuse for 30 minutes. Remove the vanilla pod and mix with the remaining cream and sugar in a bowl. Whip lightly. Transfer to a serving dish. Decorate the figs, then serve with the cream.

ROSE-FLAVOURED ICE CREAM

Not strictly a traditional Middle Eastern recipe, but a delicious way of using Turkish delight. Serve scattered with rose petals, if you have them.

4 egg yolks
115g/4oz/½ cup caster sugar
300ml/½ pint/1¼ cups milk
300ml/½ pint/1¼ cups double cream
15ml/1 tbsp rose water
175g/6oz rose-flavoured Turkish delight, chopped

SERVES 6

1 Beat the egg yolks and sugar until light. In a pan, bring the milk to the boil. Add to the egg and sugar, stirring, then return to the pan.

2 Continue stirring over a low heat until the mixture coats the back of a spoon. Do not boil, or it will curdle. Leave to cool, then stir in the cream and rose water.

3 Put the Turkish delight in a pan with 30–45ml/2–3 tbsp water. Heat gently, until almost completely melted, with just a few small lumps. Remove from the heat and stir into the cool custard mixture.

4 Leave the mixture to cool completely, then pour into a shallow freezer container. Freeze for 3 hours until just frozen all over. Spoon the mixture into a bowl.

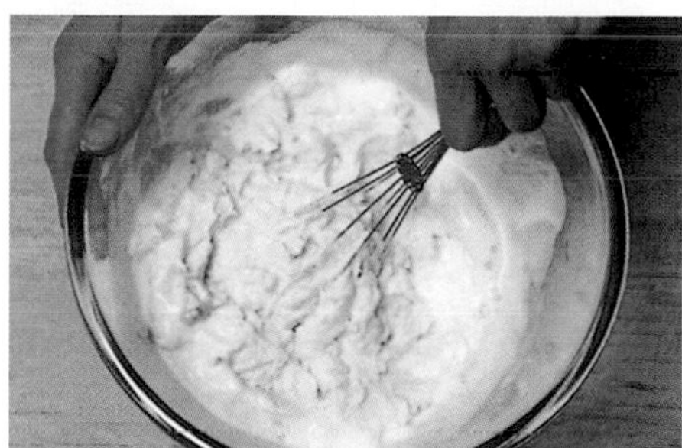

5 Using a whisk, beat the mixture well, and return to the freezer container and freeze for 2 hours more. Repeat the beating process, then return to the freezer for about 3 hours, or until firm. Remove the ice cream from the freezer 20–25 minutes before serving. Serve with thin almond biscuits or meringues.

HONEY AND PINE NUT TART

Honey of all kinds is produced throughout Greece and Turkey and provides the classic sweet taste of Eastern Mediterranean desserts.

FOR THE PASTRY
225g/8oz/2 cups plain flour
115g/4oz/½ cup butter
30ml/2 tbsp icing sugar
1 egg

FOR THE FILLING
115g/4oz/½ cup unsalted butter, diced
115g/4oz/½ cup caster sugar
3 eggs, beaten
175g/6oz/⅔ cup sunflower or other flower honey
grated rind and juice of 1 lemon
225g/8oz/2⅔ cups pine nuts
pinch of salt
icing sugar for dusting

SERVES 6

1 Preheat the oven to 180°C/350°F/Gas 4. Sift the flour into a bowl, add the butter and work with your fingertips until the mixture resembles fine breadcrumbs. Stir in the icing sugar. Add the egg and 15ml/1 tbsp of water and work to a firm dough that leaves the bowl clean.

2 Roll out the pastry on a floured surface and use to line a 23cm/9in tart tin. Prick the base with a fork, and chill for 10 minutes. Line with foil or greaseproof paper and fill with dried beans or rice, or baking beans if you have them. Bake the tart shell for 10 minutes.

3 Cream together the butter and caster sugar until light. Beat in the eggs one by one. Gently heat the honey in a small saucepan until runny, then add to the butter mixture with the lemon rind and juice. Stir in the pine nuts and salt, then pour the filling into the pastry case.

4 Bake for about 45 minutes, until the filling is lightly browned and set. Leave to cool slightly in the tin, then dust generously with icing sugar. Serve warm, or at room temperature, with crème fraîche or vanilla ice cream.

DATE AND ALMOND TART

Fresh dates make an unusual but delicious filling for a tart. The influences here are French and Middle Eastern – a true Mediterranean fusion!

FOR THE PASTRY

175g/6oz/1½ cups plain flour
75g/3oz/6 tbsp butter
1 egg

FOR THE FILLING

90g/3½oz/scant ½ cup butter
90g/3½oz/7 tbsp caster sugar
1 egg, beaten
90g/3½oz/scant 1 cup ground almonds
30ml/2 tbsp plain flour
30ml/2 tbsp orange flower water
12–13 fresh dates, halved and stoned
60ml/4 tbsp apricot jam

SERVES 6

1 Preheat the oven to 200°C/400°F/Gas 6. Place a baking sheet in the oven. Sift the flour into a bowl, add the butter and work with your fingertips until the mixture resembles fine breadcrumbs. Add the egg and a tablespoon of cold water, then work to a smooth dough.

2 Roll out the pastry on a lightly floured surface and use to line a 20cm/8in tart tin. Prick the base with a fork, then chill until needed.

3 To make the filling, cream the butter and sugar until light, then beat in the egg. Stir in the ground almonds, flour and 15ml/1 tbsp of the orange flower water, mixing well.

4 Spread the mixture evenly over the base of the pastry case. Arrange the dates, cut side down, on the almond mixture. Bake on the hot baking sheet for 10–15 minutes, then reduce the heat to 180°C/350°F/Gas 4. Bake for a further 15–20 minutes until light golden and set.

5 Transfer the tart to a rack to cool. Gently heat the apricot jam, then press through a sieve. Add the remaining orange flower water.

6 Brush the tart with the jam and serve at room temperature.

SEMOLINA AND NUT HALVA

Semolina is a popular ingredient in many desserts and pastries in the Eastern Mediterranean. Here it provides a spongy base for soaking up a deliciously fragrant spicy syrup.

FOR THE HALVA

115g/4oz/½ cup unsalted butter, softened
115g/4oz/½ cup caster sugar
finely grated rind of 1 orange, plus 30ml/2 tbsp juice
3 eggs
175g/6oz/1 cup semolina
10ml/2 tsp baking powder
115g/4oz/1 cup ground hazelnuts

TO FINISH

350g/12oz/1½ cups caster sugar
2 cinnamon sticks, halved
juice of 1 lemon
60ml/4 tbsp orange flower water
50g/2oz/½ cup unblanched hazelnuts, toasted and chopped
50g/2oz/½ cup blanched almonds, toasted and chopped
shredded rind of 1 orange

SERVES 10

1 Preheat the oven to 220°C/425°F/Gas 7. Grease and line the base of a deep 23cm/9in square solid-based cake tin.

2 Lightly cream the butter in a bowl. Add the sugar, orange rind and juice, eggs, semolina, baking powder and hazelnuts and beat the ingredients together until smooth.

3 Turn into the prepared tin and level the surface. Bake for 20–25 minutes until just firm and golden. Leave to cool in the tin.

4 To make the syrup, put the sugar in a small heavy-based saucepan with 575ml/18fl oz/2¼ cups water and the half cinnamon sticks. Heat gently, stirring, until the sugar has dissolved completely.

5 Bring to the boil and boil fast, without stirring, for 5 minutes. Measure half the boiling syrup and add the lemon juice and orange flower water to it. Pour over the halva. Reserve the remainder of the syrup in the pan.

6 Leave the halva in the tin until the syrup is absorbed then turn it out on to a plate and cut diagonally into diamond-shaped portions. Scatter with the nuts.

7 Boil the remaining syrup until slightly thickened then pour it over the halva. Scatter the shredded orange rind over the cake and serve with lightly whipped or clotted cream.

COOK'S TIP

Be sure to use a deep solid-based cake tin, rather than one with a loose base, otherwise the syrup might seep out.

INDEX